PRAISE FOR *HANDLE WITH CARE*

"Over the past half century, becoming a physician has changed dramatically—or has it? In *Handle with Care: A Doctor's Search for Faith, Fact, and Feeling*, prominent cardiologist Dr. Milton Klein reflects on how his medical training transformed him from a wide-eyed university student to a seasoned and reflective physician. The way he openly shares his triumphs and struggles from medical school through medical practice and how these shaped him as a doctor will doubtless touch any reader. While technological advances and other forces over the past fifty years have changed the face of medicine, many timeless and universal challenges await any budding physician today—and no one describes this better than Dr. Klein."

— Thomas G. Keens, MD
Professor of Pediatrics, Physiology, and Neuroscience
Keck School of Medicine of the University of Southern California
Member, Charter Class of the UCSD School of Medicine, 1968–1972

"With graceful and elegant prose, Dr. Klein takes us on an educational and entertaining journey through his fifty-year medical career as a distinguished cardiologist. Along the way, we learn how medical students and doctors worked and thought then and now, how medicine has evolved, and how it might go forward. Overall, a rewarding read for both patients and medical professionals."

— Sheldon Rubenfeld, MD, FACP
Clinical Professor, Baylor College of Medicine
Executive Director, Center for Medicine after the Holocaust

"Here is the fascinating account of a physician's personal, erudite medical journey, as well as the many changes in medical education and clinical practice he observed along the way. Dr. Klein's retrospective details with affection the sublime wisdom of his mentors while reminding us of the humor in our medical education. His narrative will prompt any physician to reflect on their own medical experience and enlighten the nonphysician to the universal human experience in the noble pursuit of healthcare."

— Eric Haufrect, MD
Past President of the Medical Staff, Houston Methodist Hospital

HANDLE WITH CARE

Also by Milton S. Klein
Learned by Heart: Dialogues with My Father

HANDLE WITH CARE

A Doctor's Search for
Faith, Fact, and Feeling

Milton S. Klein, MD

Copyright © 2022 by Milton S. Klein

All rights reserved. In accordance with the US Copyright Act of 1976, without limiting the rights under copyright reserved above, no part of this publication may be reproduced, stored in, or introduced into a retrieval system, or transmitted, in any form or by any means (electronic, mechanical, photocopying, recording, or otherwise) without the prior written permission of the copyright holder and the publisher of this book, with the exception of brief quotations embodied in critical articles or reviews.

ISBN: 978-1-956470-62-8 (hardcover)
ISBN: 978-1-956470-63-5 (paperback)
ISBN: 978-1-956470-64-2 (e-book)
LIBRARY OF CONGRESS CONTROL NUMBER 2022917200

PUBLISHED BY
Redwood Publishing, LLC
www.redwooddigitalpublishing.com
Orange County, California

COPYEDITING
Kate Zentall, Los Angeles, California

LAYOUT AND COVER DESIGN
Glenn Wong, GW Graphic Works
Los Angeles, California

To purchase copies from the author directly or in bulk for use in conferences, seminars, and/or workshops, please contact the author directly at:
mkleinauthor@gmail.com

To Gail, Josh, and Stephen.
You have my whole heart.

CONTENTS

PREFACE *ix*

1. A FISH STORY   1
2. PREMEDITATED PREMED   9
3. WELCOME TO THE "CHARGER" CLASS   15
4. STUDENTS THEN AND NOW   21
5. IT IS BETTER TO GIVE THAN TO RECEIVE   27
6. THE BODY OF INFORMATION: WHEN ANATOMY IS GROSS   37
7. A RAT'S TALE   41
8. TRANSLATING LIFE THROUGH THE LENS OF SCIENCE   51
9. THE SNAKE, THE HORNED TOAD, AND THE IGUANA   59
10. A FEW LOOSE SCREWS   67
11. HISTORY TAKING: A HEARING TEST FOR THE DOCTOR   73
12. LET'S GET PHYSICAL   89
13. "IF YOU CAN'T GET ALL YOUR WORK DONE IN TWENTY-FOUR HOURS, YOU JUST HAVE TO STAY UP LATE"   101

Contents

14. Sisyphus, Hercules, or Job: Was It All Too Much to Ask? 111

15. The EMR Billing Platform and a Plea for More Common Cents 123

16. The Fault, Dear Brutus, Is Not in Our Healthcare System, But in Ourselves 137

17. It Serves You Right 153

18. How to Change Your Mind 163

19. Compassion vs. Empathy 171

20. The Bad News Bearers 181

21. Faith and Medicine: Is the Doctor the Only God in the House? 189

22. Trending Now: The Wrap-Up 205

Acknowledgments 215

PREFACE

Although most of my medical-school generation has long eschewed belief in witchcraft, unicorns, potions, and poltergeists, all would agree that there was truly a time when the Giants walked the earth. Oh, I am not referring to the Jurassic period, when the ponderous footsteps of dinosaurs shook the riverbanks, or when Zeus hurled thunderbolts from atop Mount Olympus. Nor in the world of medicine does this allude to those soppy days when TV-America was drooling over Dr. Kildare, bullied by Ben Casey, revolted by Gregory House, or anesthetized by Marcus Welby—all of whom pretended to exude either the passionate or compassionate side of the healing arts. In truth, none of these impersonators even marginally simulated the aura, the mystique, the awesome power of the real Giants: the department chairs of medical schools. Sometimes the subject of legend, often the object of caricature, those Giants fell just short of trading card status. Variably friendly or fierce, they inspired or terrified, healed or eviscerated, spearheaded or beheaded, but always, always taught indelibly.

So much about the skills we honed, the ethic we applied, the tenacity we displayed, and the aptitude and attitude we brought to a patient's bedside was molded by the Giants. Yet this book is not an homage to the dead or dying art of intimidation; neither is it a longing for the golden days of yore of medical training. It is simply a telling of tales, medical war stories from deep in the foxhole, from the cavernous pit of the body cavity—some absurd, some gruesome, some tender—that help to trace the almost ineffable transition from college student to doctor. Who chooses such a journey, who guides them along the way, and which itinerary they select may help explain how these travelers have come to change the way we interface with them today.

Less often the focus of literary or dramatic attention than, say, that of the resident or graduate physician, the tumultuous, confusing, awkward, exhausting, and often ulcerogenic life of the medical student has been only infrequently revealed to general audiences.

Perhaps more than with any other professional, the naive medical student requires in his training a constant retooling of language and technical skills vital to his future management of risk and crisis. And then there is always the dreaded bell-shaped curve, with its implicit, guilt-laden seduction that lures students into making what should be logical clinical decisions. The outcomes of statistical outliers occasionally lead to a tortured and often macabre dance with pain or death. Far more unbearable than the comparatively trivial discomfort of dealing with the sight of blood, the greater intrusion on the student's sensibility is the struggle with the consequences of a clinical error and the accompanying neurosis from which he may never recover. Almost masochistically, this obsessive mental baggage is often mercilessly unpacked nightly.

Until fifty years ago, our fossilized medical school curriculum had remained in place for centuries. That is not to imply the absence of updates as science progressed, but rather that the *methods* of teaching had petrified. Then, in the late 1960s, something began to stir. As the population aged and expanded and as the predictions of a doctor shortage became prophetic, new schools suddenly burgeoned. Those yearning to be healers still dreamed their dreams, and the Giants still tattooed their differential diagnoses on the raw flesh of their young idolizers, but their once glacial approach to teaching began to thaw.

In 1968, ours was a new and altogether innovative program of study compared with the typical curriculum. For the first time, computer science became a core discipline, first-year students were introduced to the wards, and the basic sciences were taught by clinical faculty bridging the chasm between didactic lectures in pathology and physiology and real patients with real diseases. Anatomy instruction was placed in the hands of radiologists and surgeons rather than anatomists to highlight clinical practicality.

As one who trained in the 1960s at the crossroads between an ancient Hippocratic code and the critical thinking required to manipulate the new explosive technologies of computer and genetic science, I have worked to keep a foot in both arenas. Time constraints and changing attitudes, however, have played havoc with a patient's expectations and a doctor's sense of obligation. I maintain, for example, that today's "concierge physician" is identical to whom we used to simply call "doctor."

Now, fifty years later, a convergence of factors has forged the creation of a different generation of physician—the so-called healthcare provider. This new nomenclature announced a metamorphosis that has not gone unnoticed by patients old enough to compare the before with the after. The forces that shaped many of the changes we now encounter—in child rearing, medical student selection, Accreditation Council of Graduate Medical Education restrictions, electronic medical records, telemedicine, government policy, and reimbursement strategies, among others—play pivotal roles in reconfiguring the profession and the demeanor of the healthcare provider.

There may be no honest way to explain my fifty-year experience in healthcare delivery without appearing to sound judgmental. Despite my best attempts to avoid bias and objectively balance the advantages and disadvantages of several paths to medical practice, I cannot help but be burdened by the singular history with which I am most familiar and which complicates my impartiality.

The goals of this book are twofold: first, to offer insights to the unique metamorphosis that takes place during the years of medical school training; and second, to consider some of the currents that have caused the practice of medicine to drift in new, sometimes less personal though more efficient, directions.

Preferring to avoid an academic, data-driven analysis, I have chosen instead to interweave observations culled from personal vignettes and those of colleagues spanning several decades of training. I will, however, use some statistics to address the frequently quoted yet prickly assertion that our American system of medicine is "broken," applying some of the same tools of critical thinking learned in school to determine causality. With this approach, I hope to help readers understand more fully what it felt like to be a student gestating in the womb of yesteryear's training programs, and how the many changing factors that combine to characterize today's experience presage the new normal of our current doctor-patient relationship.

Many of today's doctors were turned on to their calling by a high school biology teacher, mentored by a college professor, or inspired by a family physician. Others were driven to heal the intense emotional wounds left by a disease that consumed a family member or shattered a friend. In the late 1960s, a handful preferred to endure the rigors of medical school over the insanity of conscription and the terrifying thought of an ambush in the jungles of Vietnam.

This is where it began for me.

CHAPTER 1

A FISH STORY

"What do you want to be when you grow up?" my mother pried gently with a coy smile when I was four years old. Folding dollops of ricotta cheese and raisins into plump blintz packages, she inquired this casually, pretending to be more absorbed with the salvos of hot oil sputtering from the frying pan than with my answer.

"A sturgeon," I responded confidently.

I can only assume that I had heard the two near homonyms spoken in some mixed context and concluded that each referred to the cool guy with the mask and the scalpel. Still, given my eagerness to collect rocks and examine bugs, had I then been aware that handwashing was a prerequisite for this specialty, I might have reconsidered. Fully understanding my intent and more than satisfied with my answer, my mother never again broached the subject. Once the verbal contract had been ratified, it would have been futile of me to rescind a Jewish mother's dream.

I won't deny that I really did prefer wearing either the clown or the mariachi costume for Halloween even more than the surgical scrubs and white coat, but the look on my mother's face when I dressed up as the doctor was hard to ignore. Despite my young age, I must have intuited that a life in the circus or playing guitar in a Mexican restaurant would have afforded a limited future compared with a career in medicine. Fortunately, since I never seriously entertained an alternative, and having concluded that becoming a sturgeon was not a viable option, there was now only the matter of selecting the school. While the goal was clear to me at the time, I had yet to map the terrain I would traverse to attain it. A wide expanse of biology and honing of skills lay ahead to make that dream come true.

Curiosity: An Introduction to Science

I WAS A PAINFULLY SLOW EATER, utterly frustrating my father, who inhaled his food as if someone were conspiring to steal his plate (a habit ingrained during the pogroms he experienced in Hungary as a child). My agonizingly slow grazing tempo was due less to my dislike of food than to my fascination with anatomy. I liked to trace the pathways of the veins as they coursed into the armpit of a chicken wing and examine its joint articulations. The neck bones were especially intriguing; their intricate shapes and interlocking structures seemed almost too clever for evolutionary serendipity, and their elegant mechanical cooperation nearly convinced me to consider studying neurosurgery in the future. Ultimately, I was left alone at the table, the other members of my family having completed their meal while I lingered engrossed in dissection. I would like to believe that my disdain for vegetables had something to do with their absence of obvious organs or moving parts.

Nourishing my penchant for science, my parents purchased the plastic models of the Invisible Grasshopper, Invisible Dog, and Invisible Man, moving up the phylogenetic chain as if to mimic Genesis. Years later I wondered why they had chosen to skip the model of the Invisible Woman, but then realized their decision may have been dictated by the premarital sexual prohibitions of Jewish orthodoxy. Unfazed and sensing no deprivation, I dissected a random array of things, many of which were not kosher: frogs, worms, grasshoppers, mice, roadkill, even the occasional bird my dog, Cindy, caught and brought me as a goodwill offering.

Beginning in sixth grade, our family doctor would invite me back to his office to discuss medicine and encourage my career plans. There was always something special, magical about sitting in the inner sanctum of his office, the faint must of old textbooks clinging to the air, displacing the scent of alcohol swabs from the exam rooms. Unquestionably, I preferred the former. I absorbed our serious, intimate conversations with utmost sobriety, noting his polished but kind bedside manner and reflecting on his years of service. I was not convinced yet that I would ever match those skills, but during late-night visions, I entertained my own private, wild aspirations. His voice was soft and measured, ever articulate. I noticed how the backs of his hands were smooth and hairless, the result, I assumed, of a life of vigorous presurgical handwashing.

For my birthday, my doctor presented me with subscriptions to *Natural History* magazine and *Scientific American*, deriving great pleasure from my discoveries and enthusiasm. How could someone so antiseptic be so warm and encouraging? I wondered. Many years later, he placed his office schedule on hold for three days to travel out of state to attend my White Coat Ceremony. From time to time thereafter, I sent him scientific papers I had written, imagining his satisfaction at having contributed in some measure to my success. He was, for me, the real Marcus Welby.

Resisting Arrest

In 1961, after I completed seventh grade, we moved to Mexico City. And it was at this young age that I had my first real taste of clinical cardiology. On a Sabbath afternoon, following our usual large lunch and in front of the family, my father stood up from the table, walked tentatively over to the couch in the living room, glazed over for a moment, teetered, and then collapsed in cardiac arrest. He was fifty-two. I was nearly thirteen years old and remember being frozen in my tracks as I watched the spectacle in horror. No single muscle flexed, no brain cell fired; I was numb—lost in time as if paralyzed, captive to a hypnotic spell. Those few excruciating minutes were replayed in slow motion in my mind during many ensuing years of self-flagellation. I clearly could not be counted on; I served no purpose. I may even have gotten in the way, an impediment, a liability like a fractured arm in a sling; in short, I did nothing. Quick-witted and moving swiftly, my mother tossed a glass of water in my father's face and miraculously, he awoke. I now know that he probably converted himself spontaneously from deadly ventricular tachycardia back to normal sinus rhythm.

My father, a rabbi, had been beckoned by the Jewish Theological Seminary to establish the first Conservative synagogue in Mexico. Anxious to avoid panic among the members of my father's new congregation, his doctors elected to set up a mini-CCU in our apartment rather than send him to the hospital. (In fact, the first CCU would not be invented until the mid-1960s, in Kansas City). They believed they could better control the details of the story, at least the one they eventually planted and pruned. My father's primary cardiologist was Dr. Teodoro Cesarman, a world-renowned medical figure and the official physician to López Mateos, the president of Mexico.

With a knowing smile and exquisite clinical finesse, Dr. Cesarman first placed his gentle hand and then his stethoscope on my father's chest. I know he was listening intently for the reliable "lub-dub," but I think he was also studying my own anxious, tormented face as I leaned forward straining for signs of hopeful news. His face poised close to mine to fix my attention, he turned to me, and then with his soft Mexican whisper asked if I would like to learn to perform an EKG. Desperate to play a role in the healing, I leapt at the offer.

We practiced several times positioning the small suction cups in an array across my father's chest in just the prescribed spots until I felt marginally confident. Observing my concentration and my trembling yet determined fingers, my father watched with quiet encouragement and limpid blue eyes and thanked the doctor with his grateful glance. I was in medical school before I completely appreciated the subtlety of this non-verbal communication between my father and his doctor—an offering by the doctor of the kind of grace I later strove to emulate. For the next two weeks, my job was to perform daily EKGs during my father's "hospitalization," and as I think about it now, he and I convalesced together.

This trauma did not immediately derail my childhood intention to pursue the field of "sturgery." It would have been folly, however, to discount the karma of having been assigned a cardiologist as my advisor on my first day of medical school. His first piece of advice: Abandon a potential career in surgery and redirect attention to the one complex, fabulous organ that exhibits sound, movement, and electricity. I am reluctant to discount celestial intervention in my decision since I am, after all, a rabbi's son. So for quite some time I believed that choosing cardiology may not have been entirely within my control.

I waited thirty-one years for a reprieve from the feeling of helplessness that afternoon in Mexico City. My parents were living in Fort Lauderdale and I in Houston. Early one morning I received a phone call from my father's cardiologist, a recent graduate of the Miami Heart Institute with supposedly bona fide credentials. He announced that my father was in the ER having suffered a heart attack and was now in persistent atrial fibrillation. Upon hanging up the phone, I promptly called my sister.

We shared a frenetic taxi ride to the airport, landed in Florida, and drove directly from baggage claim to the hospital. All told, we arrived within five hours of our frightening phone call. Incredibly, my father was still in the ER, but more unbelievably, his arrhythmia was not as advertised. He was in persistent ventricular tachycardia—a rhythm far less stable and undoubtedly producing far more extensive heart damage than the condition his doctor had initially misdiagnosed.

I confronted the cardiologist with the revised diagnosis and EKG evidence. A look of acquiescence and despair crossed his face, his shoulders rounded, and eyes fixated on the floor. I fired him on the spot.

The understandably anxious hospital administrator offered me emergency hospital privileges to assume my father's care (despite the fact that I did not possess a license to practice medicine in the State of Florida!). Writing twelve pages of notes, revising his orders, converting his arrhythmia to normal—this time I did save his life. Given the magnitude of his heart damage, my father recuperated slowly. But six months later and despite congestive heart failure, he rallied enough to fly to Houston to officiate at our oldest son's bar mitzvah. Apparently, the threat of missing this singular event was one of the most gnawing thoughts that plagued him in his first few hours in the ER. My father maintained that surviving to attend this sacred family ceremony was one of the greatest gifts he had ever received. He died twelve months later.

The Training Begins

HAVING ALIGNED THE STARS EARLY ON, I was now, as a young teen, free to focus on optimizing future medical school applications and begin to imagine myself wearing surgical scrubs. In ninth grade I wrote away for school brochures and practiced tying knots with either hand. Serendipitously, my determination to start piano lessons at age ten to improve my dexterity was soon augmented by a true love for music.

The opportunity to quench both thirsts came when we moved to Canada during my junior year of high school. An eighty-year-old retired general practitioner who had recently lost his wife of nearly sixty years still had two season tickets to the symphony for Sunday matinees. I was delighted to accompany him to these weekly concerts, especially since he always brought with him a stack of old copies of the *New England Journal of Medicine*. I read through them haltingly, underlined words I did not understand, looked them up in a tattered medical dictionary, and started a file of medical terms. I could have asked my friend for their definitions, but I worried that his fading memory would disappoint him. That he occasionally needed help in finding his usual seats at our weekly concerts hinted at the subversive malady I chose not to expose.

In my senior year of high school, I was offered the chance to take three-hour "enrichment" classes in biology two evenings a week at the University of Alberta. The college professor was a definite uptick from my substitute biology teacher, who taught chemistry in real life and was merely filling in for the year. As the surrogate, the high school teacher was anointed with only a sprinkling of knowledge of biology, keeping precariously only one textbook chapter ahead of the class at a time. I am quite sure it was he who recommended me for this special university program, since he struggled to answer any question I posed to him from three chapters ahead and was understandably relieved to be rid of me. And for my part, relying solely on the substitute to teach my favorite subject would have been almost intolerable.

The college classroom contained a riotous display of specimens, graphs, and formulas related to invertebrate life. Long segments (called proglottids) of tapeworms were dissected and suspended in formaldehyde jars, their anatomical parts identified with pins. In the enrichment classes, we studied the detailed pathology of ten round, unsegmented worms (the nematodes) and the human diseases they imparted. The longer their scientific names, the more I reveled in them. Clearly this was the highlight of my high school experience, and I could feel myself inching closer to my future profession. So comprehensive was the information covered in this class that nothing new was added when I revisited the diseases caused by these worms during my medical school pathology course four years later.

CHAPTER 2

PREMEDITATED PREMED

I ENROLLED AT MCGILL UNIVERSITY in Montreal as a sophomore, with a dual major in zoology (biology) and chemistry. Many of my professors lectured in cap and gown, cloaked in old-world auras, and many students wore sport coats to class. Adhering to a British system of education in 1965, McGill offered few semester courses; almost all classes lasted the entire year. Since medical schools in the United States required at least one quarter each of several courses in chemistry and biology, I was obliged to cram seven full years of chemistry classes into three years of college. The upside to this was having to learn to assimilate large masses of information for the final exam, which became invaluable when studying for national board exams in later years.

Many of my advanced zoology lectures (microbiology and comparative anatomy, among others) were held in the austere, heavily-ivied medical school buildings. I especially loved the old gray stone turrets and crenellations of the Royal Victoria Hospital. Here, in the institution that gave voice in the late 1800s to the father of modern medicine, Sir William Osler (later to become one of the four founders of the Johns Hopkins School of Medicine), I roamed the halls, gentian violet stains like Rorschach tests splattered over my lab coat. Dappled light filtering through wavy glass windows pockmarked the wooden desks that once witnessed some of the greatest lecturers in neurobiology: Wilder Penfield, Theodore Rasmussen, and Ronald Melzack. As the pungent "Eau de Formalin" perfume oozed from the dissection benches into my clothing, I smeared bacterial colonies onto petri dishes, stacked and labeled them neatly into their incubators, and allowed myself the fantastic pretense that I could be discovering a cure that might someday save humankind. My trudging up University Street in -30 degrees F at 5:00 p.m. in the dark of winter and rounding the last corner stung by a heartless wind tunnel added a mantle of martyrdom to my devotion to science.

Trials and Errors

WITH LIMITED EXTRACURRICULAR HOURS available to me, I cleared some time to participate in the enormously popular Premed Society. It was in one of the larger hospital auditoriums that I first heard a lecture from the famous cardiac surgeon Dr. Arthur Vineberg. In his presentation, he outlined his new surgical triumph, named (no surprise) the Vineberg Procedure, designed to treat coronary artery disease and its attendant symptom of angina. Experimenting first on animals starting in 1946, Dr. Vineberg ultimately performed this operation on thousands of patients with severe chest pain. The surgery involved opening the patient's chest, severing the end of the internal mammary artery, and stuffing the blunt end of the artery into the area of the heart deprived of blood supply due to coronary blockages. He believed this procedure would stimulate new blood vessel growth in the diseased region of the heart.

Despite his early reports of promising results in the postoperative control of chest pain, Dr. Vineberg's procedure was largely shunned by the wider medical community. Some of his colleagues' skepticism derived from perceived flaws in Vineberg's study design, with its few objective markers of success other than a patient's subjective description of relief of pain. Initially, other investigators reported mixed results when comparing the Vineberg Procedure with a sham operation—suggesting a strong placebo effect as the cause for improvement.

At the time, my preoccupation with these studies had little to do with my limited knowledge of the disease state, the medical value of this operation, or any other treatment option, for that matter; I was, after all, a mere chemistry-biology major, not a doctor. Yet I was stunned to hear that any patient might be willing to sign up for a sham operation. To be precise, patients with severe heart disease agreed to become control guinea pigs to ascertain the efficacy of the Vineberg Procedure—to have their chests opened, their hearts exposed, their pericardial membranes incised, and then their chests closed without receiving any real therapy that might treat their angina. In an era when scientists struggled to define success, to compare study results with adequate controls, to identify targets that were measurable, the bravery of these patients struck me in a profound way.

This kind of experimentation would be unthinkable today, when institutional review boards assigned to schools or hospitals would never consent to such sham operations. And yet the few patients who offered their bodies to science (then and since, in so many other laboratories) left a legacy that saved a much larger population from therapies that would prove unworthy. They provided the foundation for the very birth of evidence-based medicine—a field many today would be shocked to learn is surprisingly new, its first real footprint set only in the mid-1980s. While subsequent studies did confirm a limited value to the Vineberg Procedure, the advent of a more robust method to reestablish blood flow with coronary artery bypass surgery sounded Vineberg's moratorium.

This, my earliest introduction to controlled human experimentation, demanded some sorting out in my mind. First I wondered about its legality; second, about its morality; and third, where it rested along a very narrow spectrum of Hippocrates's ancient instructions to us. Who, I asked myself, is supposed to be responsible for *Primum non nocere*—First do no harm—the only admonition I had already memorized? And yet, even today that kind of research offers a perspective on the courage displayed by patients who enroll in medical trials at great personal risk.

For example, in 2019 a journal reported that a selection of women with early stages of breast cancer agreed to have a mastectomy with or without follow-up chemotherapy, despite the current standard of care that included chemotherapy. They were randomly assigned to one or the other group based on whether they had a certain genetic marker. The index group (those not taking chemotherapy) potentially exposed themselves to the spread of cancer if the gene turned out not to be protective—a life decision that, while benefitting medical science and thousands of subsequent patients, was a gamble imperiling those brave individuals participating in the protocol.

I contemplated how these patients, never identified, receive no medals, no standing ovations at ballparks. Their medical histories are concealed, their fates remain private, and their sacrifices are rarely celebrated. Perhaps the last and most vital gift to their suffering successors is the knowledge gleaned from the unique configuration of their bodies' duels with a specific illness. As I squinted at the faint shadow of my future profession, I dwelled heavily on this: These were the kinds of people I might treat someday—sometimes desperate, their nails scratching on the walls of their medical prisons, sometimes serene, determined to confront their illness head on and prepared to sacrifice everything if need be. These were the ones whose stories would fill me and consume me.

Math and Other Miseries

Despite the subzero temperature outside my dormitory, I often awoke in a sweat about getting into medical school, anguishing over the possibility that I might be accepted nowhere. For me, there had never been a plan B, no second-career choice. I envied friends who seemed willing to settle for alternatives and pitied those who anguished over career choices they had still not even identified. One of my friends who aced many of his most challenging advanced-level science courses was awarded a D grade in his elective Russian class and was rejected by twenty-eight medical schools. So it was clear that everything—everything—counted. For me, organic chemistry, the most common stumbling block for many hopeful premed students, was never a problem; I'd taken two years of it and passed handily. On the other hand, physical chemistry, crystal field theory, and quantitative analysis stood before me as Cerberus or Hydra, the multiheaded beasts. From the moment I entered the p. chem. classroom, I sensed that I was in serious trouble. Even my slide rule was too puny to compare with those of other, far more capable students.

None of the very first math equations I saw scribbled on the blackboard made sense to me, possibly because I enrolled in the course without having taken its prerequisite (a feature of the educational system at McGill that trusted in the mature decisions of its students and refused to protect them from themselves). Of course, the other explanation was that I was never comfortable in math.

Over the entire year's course, I can remember only one moment that interrupted the misery. Always arriving slightly late to class was a curvaceous blond student who never failed to wear a tight-fitting neon-colored sweater. She routinely sashayed toward the front and center of the auditorium, turning innocently around to spotlight every angle and, like thick maple syrup, pour herself slowly into her seat. The entire male section of the class and the middle-aged professor momentarily ignored their slide rules to observe this ritual. One day the professor launched a pop quiz that not only took everyone by surprise but crushed almost every student in the class.

"Well, how did you all like my little quizzy?" hissed the professor with a smile akin to the serpent's from the Garden of Eden.

"Geez!" the blond bombshell casually replied. "If that was just one of your quizzies, I'd like to see your testies!"

Class dismissed.

I was comforted only by the assumption that this material was *immaterial* to my becoming a doctor; it was just another trial, another crawl on my stomach over broken glass toward my dream. For the latter course, quantitative analysis, I relied on the premise that luck *is* in fact a strategy. Anyone who has ever had to weigh the yields from their chemical reaction on a laboratory scale with accuracy to the fourth decimal place in milligrams understands what I'm talking about. A few of those two final grades dangled dangerously from a thin filament and were the primary sources of my apprehension.

For as long as I can remember, I have observed how it has always seemed that when I approach a crossroads in my life, a letter arrives in the mail, telling me exactly what to do. And true to form, this time would be no exception.

CHAPTER 3

WELCOME TO THE "CHARGER" CLASS

WHO COULD HAVE POSSIBLY KNOWN what admission officers were looking for? I had not made an in-depth analysis; I was only tapping into personal observation from the perspective of an applicant. In the years before I applied, I believed that medical schools were looking for the well-rounded student whose early interest in science was obvious, whose grades reflected a facility with difficult subject material, and who had perhaps demonstrated a particle of generosity in some form of community service. By most accounts, schools with typical curricula did in fact pursue this kind of student: mostly first-born Caucasian males. Scanning the brochures from various schools I considered attending, I found that this appeared to be the emphasis, especially as I looked over the profiles of prior freshman classes.

I could not have anticipated how different the resumes were of the first entrants of the newly formed University of California San Diego School of Medicine. Neither could I have appreciated the sweeping innovations planned for the curriculum of its charter class of 1968 (the year I applied), since the school only hinted at its ultimate strategies. But I was soon to find out.

YOU'RE IN!

"WELCOME TO THE **CHARGER** CLASS," read the telegram that preceded my more formal letter of acceptance. At first I was understandably confused.

I was already a fan of the San Diego Chargers football team, but I did not for one moment believe they would consider me a candidate for the squad. I became even more skeptical when I realized that the school I had dreamed about attending, the one that would infuse my brain with an entire field of medicine over the next four years, had mistyped the most important message of my life!

The Charter Class was, however, special. Of the entering forty-seven students, thirty-two had advanced degrees in other fields: some had PhDs in mathematics, others were engineers or professors of English literature—a mature, accomplished group. On average, the class was older than most, and the faculty boasted eight Nobel laureates. As the baby of the class (I was not quite twenty), I was, you can imagine, intimidated. Two of our earliest lectures were given by none other than Jonas Salk and Linus Pauling, with *The Population Bomb* author, Paul R. Ehrlich, to follow! Well, this is about where my mother stepped into the picture.

Requesting a meeting with Dr. Harold Simon, the dean of students, she sought assurances that I would be well cared for. I don't recall if I was struck by the absurdity of this proposition, or if I suspected my mother lacked confidence in my ability to compete with such polished adversaries, several of whom could have taught biochemistry themselves. She had not run interference for me in the past, so this was something of a surprise stipulation, and surprisingly I acquiesced. But she was not usually one to demand, and thus not one to be easily denied.

I sat in the book-lined office like a limp appendage as my mother engaged the dean in an initial exchange of the usual niceties, followed by a rapid-fire scherzo of more pointed questions. I tried helplessly to smile through my embarrassment, but my mortification was painfully evident. The dean, seemingly calm in the face of her interrogation, never revealed dismay, never ridiculed. My mother, meanwhile, once convinced I was in good hands and able to survive in this environment and holding the dean to a promise to oversee my sanity, gathered herself, rose from her seat, and strode out of the room.

WELCOME TO THE "CHARGER" CLASS

Yet another layer of obligation had been laid on me. I resolved to prove them all right—to survive school, of course, but more than that. Striving for grades alone suddenly became a meaningless exercise of the past. The time had come for me to examine my character, to challenge my motivation, to plumb the depth of my desire to serve—in short, to make *myself* proud. As yet unaware of just what it would take for me—or my classmates, for that matter—to train these compulsions into becoming the best I could be, I had even less insight into the forces that might impact the attitudes of students of the future, the very students I would subsequently teach.

IS THIS CALL FOR ME?

IN THOSE FIRST FEW DAYS and for many years thereafter, I was ill equipped to consider the question of what draws someone to the calling of medicine. But today, aided by decades of hindsight, I can ask: Is there really a difference in the character and mindset of students attracted to medicine who are entering school today as compared with those from back then? I don't mean to imply that modern-day bones of compassion are more osteoporotic, that knowledge is more anemic, or that dedication to service is more jaundiced today. *I truly do not believe any of that.*

I am convinced that the lure the field of medicine holds for most students has always been the same. The love of science, desire to heal, sense of duty and empathy, and the vehicle for community service—all have their magnetic pull. A colleague reflected on his first impressions of what the medical profession represented and whom he someday hoped to emulate:

"I was about ten years old when a doctor made a house call dressed in a three-piece suit, tie, and watch chain. I remember the aura of respect, awe, and admiration he commanded, and I knew then that I wanted to be that guy and recreate that art of communication, applying it to the field of preventative medicine."

It would be naive, of course, to believe that prestige, adulation, and financial security play no role, but they are not central to a journey that costs so much in time, effort, emotion, and tuition. There are too many other ways to feed an ego and make money than through the trial by fire of medical school. A graphic example recently came to mind of what dedication in any generation looks like.

During my first year of residency, I was assigned to mentor a frail third-year student for her first twelve-week rotation on the wards. She was bright and eager but reserved and a bit mysterious in the way people refer to still waters running deep. Early one afternoon on rounds, we happened upon an elderly man who had layered the entire floor of his hospital room with bloody diarrhea before collapsing in the center of the muck in cardiac arrest. Wasting no time and without a second thought, the student threw herself onto the floor next to the patient and initiated CPR. Still wearing her street clothes now half-covered in excrement, she began vigorous chest compression and positive pressure ventilation. For others on our team, the reaction was less instantaneous, functioning as they did in a secondary role, but the effort was nonetheless heroic. Between the splash of IV fluids, sparks from the defibrillator, and horrendous odor, the patient's vital signs were restored after about thirty minutes.

Because of her, the man survived. Being pivotal during a few isolated moments of someone's life summarized the lodestone for this otherwise demure student, and probably for generations of others like her. If we are to be measured by our actions, understood by our first instincts, this young student's spontaneity argued loudly against financial incentives as her primary impetus for pursuing a career in medicine. Such are the motives of students then and now.

Lamentably, there will always be a fringe element of physicians in every generation who will corrupt the practice of medicine using the basest of principles and who do our profession no honor. Once we clear the dinner plate of those few marginal scraps, however, we can still ask if we might generalize about the generation of millennial medical students and examine if their different life experiences have instilled in them qualities, both adverse and beneficial, as future physicians that help explain the changes we encounter in today's doctor-patient interaction.

Seeking answers, I first had to contemplate the transformations that had taken place during my own generation by revisiting my early roots. Returning for my fortieth-year reunion, I asked the same much-revered dean, now frail and in his mid-nineties, whether he remembered that clumsy encounter with my mother. He paused and smiled.

"Ah, how well I remember! My father demanded the same kind of meeting with the director of admissions at the Stanford School of Medicine before my own first day of school. In a bizarre retaliation for what he felt was a sign of my immaturity, the director then rescinded my acceptance, and I had to make do with Harvard. How grateful I was that we did not make that same error with you." Dr. Simon, the most succinct yet eloquent man I ever knew, died a few months later.

When I heard about the dean's passing, I recalled the way his brilliance and wisdom could both support and intimidate. I had not been sure as a student at the time what lay ahead in the next four years, but I knew that as the adventure unfolded I would feel safer with Dr. Simon by my side.

CHAPTER 4

STUDENTS
THEN AND NOW

DELAYED GRATIFICATION became the mantra of my early medical school mindset. I accepted that years of premed science (and, ugh, math) classes were part of this trial. Upon completing my final mathematics exam in college, my celebration balloons were soon pricked when, to my utter dismay, I learned I still had to take biostatistics in medical school. Worse, we were the first to require a competency in computer science—learning to program at a GE time-sharing facility and expected to write code for our biochemistry kinetics formulae (remember, this was 1968).

I also accepted that many more years of anatomy, pathology, biochemistry, and physiology lay ahead. I especially remember the momentary blurred vision and brief pang of nausea when I perused the four-foot poster that hung at the entrance of the biochemistry laboratory. From three feet away, it appeared to be painted a light shade of gray. Approaching closer, however, I could make out a frenzy of tangled symbols, arrows, and near-microscopic writing representing the labyrinthine interrelated biochemical equations and their catalysts that propelled bodily functions known at that time. (By now, no doubt the poster has doubled in size as our knowledge has expanded.) I embraced the fact that this, too, must be learned. And yet as I homed in on a specialization in cardiology, I fully acknowledged that this landfill of information, along with skills and data related to entire fields like gynecology, ENT, pediatrics, and ophthalmology, among others accumulated over the years, would ultimately be sidelined and forgotten. I would be expected to endure a multiyear hazing ritual before gaining entry into the fraternity of medicine. These were the bridges I had to first cross before burning them behind me.

THE BIG DIG: YESTERDAY'S LIBRARY SEARCH

GATHERING THE FACTS that exposed the body's most covert secrets was an inefficient mission and often a slow grind. Entire chapters were read to unearth a single piece of information. The *Index Medicus*, a steady library-stack companion, kept me company for hours as I tilled tangential articles to exhume the one point I sought. Two features of future-physician training were operant during this exercise: The first involved the actual work of excavation, the digging for information. Precious answers were often buried, and it was all too easy to be distracted by confusing, inaccurate, or poorly proven data and other "shiny objects." Learning to ignore the Abstract, Discussion, and Conclusion sections of a scientific paper until the Methods and Materials section was properly vetted became second nature. Gaining an intimacy with the construction of a scientific article supported the tenet that merely reading about science did not necessarily make one a scientist. The effort, endurance, critical thinking—and time, lots of time—required to slog through the information morass to unveil the truth was enormous and considered by some to be a waste of time.

The second benefit was the discovery of unrelated and often surprising gems along the way. And did we care if these data were not immediately germane to the topic under search? Not really. Sometimes these unexpected facts served as missing pieces that might eventually fit a different puzzle, proving instrumental in diagnosing the evil that lurked beneath the sheets in the adjacent hospital bed.

As upper-level students on call for thirty-six-hour intervals, we were given a key to the library in lieu of an on-call bed. This provided a respite from the chaos at 4:00 a.m. and an opportunity to prepare for Morning Report or work rounds with one's attending staff. Students and interns collected all relevant data regarding their overnight admissions. Chest x-rays, which could sometimes go astray or be appropriated by another resident reviewing them, were often hoarded so as to be available for discourse and hedge against public ridicule by the chief at Morning Report (information readily accessible on students' cellphones today). Nurses who took pity on us would lose their jobs if caught offering a weary student an unoccupied cot for an hour of sleep. Scratching, scrounging, raking for the answer, drowning ourselves in the pathophysiology, the mechanisms, the differential diagnosis… this was our premier sport; this was why, during these few years, we were placed on Earth.

With the Swipe of a Finger

Today's students, too, must hunt for information, but with the aid of far more powerful search engines intended to minimize the pain of lost time. According to Simon Sinek, a British-American lecturer, author of five books, motivational speaker, and TED presenter, millennials have a different approach to problem-solving, perhaps as a result rather than despite this technology. In his 2016 "Millennials in the Workplace" YouTube lecture, Sinek points to four elements contributing to the way millennials address and manage challenges: parental upbringing, social media (technology), instant gratification (also technology), and the corporate/professional environment. For now let us put aside the role of parenting as too individual to factor in when considering how millennials handle data acquisition (or subsequently interface with patients).

Sinek describes how students growing up swaddled by an omniscient internet expect all answers to be at their fingertips. Information is googled and instantaneous, making the lesson of digging for an answer an almost superfluous if not vestigial callisthenic. Of course, in medicine, as in so many other professions, one can effortlessly find the correct answer to the wrong question: a cure in search of a disease. The real skill is in knowing which question to ask. For the millennial, Sinek argues, time on task as a goal unto itself is not appreciated as having contemporary value. And so impatience is fed by an addiction to immediate gratification. The psycho-chemical response to uncovering an instant solution, much like that triggered by almost any cellphone social-media "ping," is driven by the very same dependency on the dopamine surge that occurs with alcohol and tobacco abuse. And yet in an environment that weighs the merit of time, whether as a doctor or as a patient, doesn't the efficiency that accrues with technology offer overwhelming advantage?

THE TRADE-OFF

EDUCATORS POINT OUT that more new information about medicine has been accumulated in the last fifty years than in all prior history. This tsunami of data may not justify or even tolerate the squandering of time needed to dredge the medical literature for a few paltry facts as was the norm in my day. Here, then, is the tradeoff in this aspect of medical school education: The old way was inefficient, ponderous, and time consuming, but like basic training for the young soldier, it added bulk to the muscles of tenacity, reinforcing habits of critical thinking and the discriminatory agility to sift through the literature by tweezing apart the worthless from the worthwhile.

It stands to reason that the current system is far less serpentine, far more focused. House staff can choose to spend this extra time with their patients or family or else even assimilate more knowledge. But all too often, driven by technical studies and relying on the precision of machinery, today's diagnosticians are apt to place less emphasis on the valuable art of the physical examination, the "laying on of hands" that can provide vital clues and direct further inquiry. Observation, palpation, percussion, and auscultation (the act of listening with a stethoscope)—these can supplement, confirm, or question the results proffered by technology, while establishing a physical connection between patient and doctor.

As for that physical connection, it too is something of an art, and one that does not spring fully formed via textbooks and lectures. And in my case, in my freshman medical school class, developing and practicing these bedside techniques often awkwardly connected students to students.

CHAPTER 5

IT IS BETTER TO GIVE
THAN TO RECEIVE

In most other graduate school environments, the first few days of orientation are usually the time for social dialogue, cross-referencing family backgrounds, identifying likes and dislikes, and maybe even sharing personal aspirations for the future. In our school, however, we kicked off the camaraderie with a friendly student-faculty game of touch football—the planning committee likely aiming for team building of some kind. Few of us were scholar-athletes, but one genetics professor had been a halfback at Ohio State, one student had played varsity football as an offensive lineman for UCLA, and yet another student had given up a professional rugby contract in Australia to attend medical school. I do not recall the score or who won, but the losers included a student with a few fractured ribs and a professor needing surgery to remove a partially damaged kidney. That was the friendly part. A few days later, the truly brutal games would begin.

The Naked Truth

Divided into groups of four students, we who had just barely exchanged names were about to get to know one another better than we'd imagined as we were ushered into exam rooms... and asked to disrobe. Each of us had already inherited a stethoscope upon arrival, although our familiarity with its use was limited to watching doctor-based television shows. I distinctly remember sitting on the edge of the examination table in my underwear, holding my new stethoscope to my chest, curious to hear my own heartbeat. Just then, the instructor peeked in the door, and with a wry smile and sarcastic wink suggested I might find it more instructive if I placed the distal end of the scope on the *patient's* chest rather than my own. Self-conscious and amused, we all went about working our clumsy way from head down to foot in as serious a manner as we could muster. We were, after all, already doing "doctor stuff," a psychological thrill in itself. Until...

The instructor exited the room leaving us with the final tasks of performing the urological and rectal exams on one another.

Fumbling and gushing apologies, we diverted our eyes as we had practiced for years while showering with our high school sports teams. We alternated our positions, turning our heads and coughing or else bending over. I had the distinct misfortune of partnering with Paul, a six-foot-four student with an enormous hand. Totally in the dark (well, really, just intellectually) as to what pathology we were investigating, this first lesson, I now believe, was aimed to conquer our discomfort with our own bodies. As a prelude to many subsequent exercises, and especially as an introduction to our upcoming anatomy lab, these tactile overtures desensitized us to far more disturbing future episodes.

At least the directors of the physical-exam curriculum had the good sense to divide the quartets according to gender; to do otherwise would have crossed the line even for inquiring minds. The men learned to do pelvic exams and the women practiced prostate exams on hospital patients who "volunteered." The awkward celebration affectionately referred to as "rectal day" at the county hospital was just another example of the bizarre but necessary passage we were to endure as freshmen. The entire class was marched down to the wards and assigned to second-level residents for direction.

Typically, an elderly male patient who was starved for extra attention and sympathetic to the need to sacrifice for medical science was singled out by the resident and asked if he would mind helping teach students how to complete a physical exam. Hopefully, the patient would be stable enough to be eased out of bed and instructed to lean over the mattress on his elbows, legs spread. The hospital gown, always tied in the back, would part ceremoniously like a stage curtain. Peering backward under his arm, the patient might prepare himself to accept the reward for his acquiescence—a line of students trailing out the door and around into the hallway, each putting on a lubricated glove. Sadly, there is no other way to learn how to interrogate the entire body, although we could have employed a little more gentility. Repelled for ourselves and frankly embarrassed for the patient, not even the boldest among us failed to apologize profusely before plumbing the plumbing. Many of us returned to visit him later that evening and in subsequent days, not only to express gratitude for his generosity but also to keep a sad patient company, someone who had traded both his privacy and dignity to assuage his loneliness. Circling back to the bedside, however, had its potential pitfalls, as divulged to me by a colleague recounting his own first patient assignment.

Close Encounters of the First Kind

THE DAY HAD FINALLY ARRIVED when he was to examine his first patient. Like most medical students, he knew enough to be fully prepared well in advance. Anticipating that he would likely be distraught and disorganized, he had written down prompts for an entire generic history and physical exam on a pad of paper with blank slots to be filled. After arriving at Charity Hospital in New Orleans, he made his way toward a large open ward with about fifteen beds crammed next to one another. There he introduced himself to an amiable, obese Black woman. That the history portion alone took two to three hours to complete is not surprising; the myriad details of a truly complete history do not distinguish the pertinent from the insignificant, and a first-year student has no experience prioritizing one from the other.

But by the time the student was finally ready to perform the physical exam, the patient was so exhausted she gently pleaded with him to return the next day. Mentally fatigued as well, he thanked the woman, accepted her request, and pledged to come back soon. Returning the following morning as promised, he began his thorough physical exam, which easily lasted another ninety minutes.

When he had finally finished, the patient asked suspiciously, "Excuse me, but exactly who are you?"

"I am the medical student who took your history yesterday," he replied, puzzled.

"No, you are not," she argued.

"Yes, I am. Don't you remember me?" he insisted.

"No," she replied with a smile now appreciating his anguish. "I just got to the hospital this morning!"

The student, so intent on producing the most complete and comprehensive write-up possible, had not even recognized this essential discrepancy—and was so embarrassed by his mistake he never confessed this oversight to his attending. Moments of hyperfocus on one task that derail the more obvious objectives are hardly uncommon for students who find themselves in such unfamiliar arenas.

I, too, recall the futility of trying to memorize all the details of the entire physical exam sequence before going in to see my first patient. The list was too long, the situation too tense, and I realized too late that I could not rely on the same powers of memory that had gotten me through college. Whenever I had to close my eyes in a desperate search for the next thing to do, I took the patient's pulse to buy time to think. After repeating this maneuver perhaps twenty times, the patient began to look concerned.

"Doctor, is there something wrong with my pulse?"

"No," I said, with a nonchalance I tried to affect. "But there is a lot of information you can learn from just the pulse." This may, in fact, have been partially true, but at that point I had absolutely no idea what that information might be.

Perhaps thirsty for a fuller breadth of knowledge and feeling emboldened, some of the more audacious female students approached three male students one evening (among whom, I recall, were the former football player and the semi-professional rugby forward) studying at the library, to ask if they might be interested in a coed experiment to learn how normal prostate and ovary organs felt. From what I recollect, the men did not take the women up on their proposition, but the fact that it was made in the first place spoke volumes on how… *stimulating* things could get in the quest for mastery, to say nothing of the need to blow off steam.

For the most part, the eight women in our class were treated fairly and without condescension from the faculty, and almost always with respect from their fellow students. I am told this treatment was a departure from the occasionally uncomfortable teasing and derision to which they were sadly subjected elsewhere back in the 1960s. A friend who graduated from the medical school in Guadalajara in that era related this anecdote about her crusty physiology professor. Apparently, this bloated, licentious old fellow would typically select a good-looking young female from the class and ask her to stand. Behind the pretense of science, he posed a series of awkward questions about the physiology of the sexual organs, gathering momentum in explicitness. His final question:

"Miss, can you tell me which muscle increases in size by a factor of seven during sexual arousal?"

"Um… the penis?" she answered hesitantly, red-faced.

"No, my dear. It is the iris, and I am afraid you are in for some real disappointment," he gloated.

I am pleased that this boorishness finds no place in medical education nowadays.

❖ ❖ ❖

I had once assumed that all curricula of my time taught physical examinations in the same "hands-on" way. Cross-referencing this experience with others, however, I recently ascertained that this overtly intimate introduction to physical examination was not typical at other schools.

As the field of medicine over the past hundred years transitioned from bloodletting in the surgical-theater-turned-barbershop and into the light of science, a dramatic evolution in the teaching of the physical examination has followed suit. I have read that at the turn of the 19th century, American medical students, in contrast with those in Germany and France, often graduated without ever having touched a patient (or even dissected a cadaver). In the 1960s, our class used itself as the first resource of examination, but by the middle of our freshman year, we had already been released onto the wards to examine real patients. A physician who was taught physical examination in a much later era, in the early 2000s, told me his school employed actors to pose as "fake patients." Even so, he described his first emotional interaction with someone he *knew* was there as a prop:

"I was so nervous and sweating, beads of sweat dropped from my forehead onto their abdomen while I performed the physical exam. I tried nonchalantly to wipe it off while doing the exam, which is hilarious in retrospect. But I imagine the sooner you start being terrible with patients as a student, the sooner you'll start getting better."

I did not ask how it was possible for an actor to simulate a large spleen, a cardiac murmur, an enlarged lymph node, a consolidated pneumonia, or a retinal hemorrhage. In highly selected cases, "professional patients" have been useful in guiding novices during their first pelvic exam, for instance, alerting students when they had not yet reached the ovary or when their manual palpation was too aggressive.

Additional lessons are instilled when a fresh-faced student walks into a hospital room unannounced and asks an ill, uncomfortable, and often reluctant patient to undress. The patient understands that this intrusion offers no value to his case; it is simply a public service to teach future doctors. For me, to have been refused by a patient and then to have to go back to the attending to ask to be assigned another candidate to examine would have been unthinkable. Balancing persistence with a charm offensive can help hone a bedside manner that might someday be useful in convincing a frightened or belligerent patient to surrender to a lifesaving procedure during an emergency.

Another colleague recalls his own first awkward examination:

"I was in the private office of a prominent internist in Dallas, and a beautiful, bountiful young lady was on the table, blouse and bra off. I was leaning over listening to her heart when my glasses fell off and onto her breast and were heaving up and down along with her breathing. I was too nervous to retrieve them. Fortunately, she had a sense of humor."

A third colleague describes a far more disturbing first exam:

"My first patient was a veteran who had attempted suicide by taking a shotgun to his jaw, succeeding in blowing his nose away so I could see his deglutition [swallowing mechanics] first-hand.... He had also separated his frontal lobe from the rest of his brain," thus destroying his emotional responses. The stark contrast between the patient's aloofness and the student's shock was palpable.

Whether horrid or humorous, it is easy to recognize the commonality of anxiety associated with the laying on of hands on the body of a stranger, even one who is not ill, not uncomfortable, and being paid to do a job. For someone barely out of college, this is still, after all, foreign ground, contradicting every social convention of respecting someone else's personal space. Students then as now learn to adapt by displacing their fears and subjugating their discomfort with the goal of becoming "less terrible" at it. They learn to compartmentalize the task. Always in the back of their mind students acknowledge that someday someone's life may depend on it.

NASAL PASSAGES: A SEARCH WITHOUT A WARRANT

MOST RECENTLY, TECHNOLOGY has varnished the experience by asking students to examine mannequins. Further removed from reality, the benefit of talking to a human being, the gift offered by a real patient, and the relief expressed by a nervous student is deferred or delayed. Perhaps because imaging has become so much more sophisticated, the teaching of the physical exam in modern medical schools has been diluted. The more

I've inquired, the more I've discovered that my own school was innovative in other unique ways as well.

Nearing the end of week two of physiology class, the chief of gastroenterology strode into the auditorium one morning with a dour sense of purpose to lecture on the secretions of the stomach. His horn-rimmed glasses, gaunt stature, umber tie, and pinstriped mahogany suit were calling cards for his subspecialty and conveyed a world of dullness. (I was yet unaware of the international esteem with which he was regarded.) I eyed with suspicion the contents of the cart resembling a tangle of squid ink linguini that he pushed before him. My awful premonition was confirmed when the chief distributed a stiff, somber-gray nasogastric tube to each member of the class and asked us to lubricate the distal end before passing it from our nose down into our own stomach. He demonstrated the technique on himself as he continued to lecture, interrupting one of his slides ever so briefly with his own slight gag reflex. This one-second gaff passed mostly unnoticed, as the cacophony of dry heaves from the majority filled the auditorium with the sounds of a chorus of sea lions at feeding time.

A student who has never endured having a nasogastric tube passed into his own stomach may not fully appreciate what it means to employ gentle technique or display maximum empathy when studying his patient. He may *believe* he does, but he will never really *know*. A mannequin will not squeal, wriggle, or complain; nor is it obese, argumentative, or unwilling to be placed in the optimal position; nor does it suffer from arthritic ailments that prevent it from assuming the proper pose. It does not look you in the eye and retch all over your white lab coat. A mannequin is not likely to be choking on its own bile at 3:00 a.m. Real-life maladies impose new challenges on students who are just now learning to start an IV or arterial line. Mannequins do not suffer from hypotension, sweating, shock, or vasoconstriction. Large artificial arteries, a steady mechanical arm, normal skin turgor, and uniform man-made anatomy all give students who are successful in learning these procedures great—but perhaps false—confidence. These issues do not make the mannequin valueless.

IT IS BETTER TO GIVE THAN TO RECEIVE

One must still admit that practicing on people, especially as an initial training, can be uncomfortable for both parties.

I do not know whether today's school curricula include students' performing complete physical examinations or starting IVs on each other or passing their own nasogastric tubes. The de-emphasis on learning to perform skilled physical examinations as well as the proliferation of sophisticated mannequins designed to replace patients may have rendered these approaches obsolete. But if so, vital lessons, both medical and emotional, may be lost.

Patients, along with doctors who themselves become patients, often relate with dismay how their physician office visits have become nontactile. Examinations, when performed, are less intense, more cursory, and superficial, bowing sometimes to the quick-triggered options for imaging, scans, and ultrasounds. While it's true that objectively directed testing of this sort may uncover some deep, important, and otherwise silent illness, it may also highlight spurious, benign, or artifactual results that send doctors and patients down a rabbit hole and expose the patient to potentially risky procedures or unnecessary costs.

Indicative of the pitfalls of the "press-one-button-and-get-a-diagnosis" solutions of thirty years ago, you may remember the exciting news about the ultimate analytical tool: the whole-body CT or MRI scan. Joint venture investors purchased the imaging equipment, installed them in eighteen-wheelers, and parked them on freeway off-ramps so drivers could conveniently stop by for a scan on their way home from work. Although not entirely without merit, this blanket approach triggered a cost—not only for the test itself but also that of a possible false diagnosis measured in unnecessary surgery, biopsies, pain, and lost productivity.

Another issue to consider when thinking about the financial implications of using duplicative and often unnecessary testing as a replacement for a careful examination was pointed out to me recently. Health-insurance carriers frequently bundle policies that cover entire families. When a parent's medical budget is depleted by indiscriminate testing, expenditures on their children's healthcare may be compromised. An example of this dilemma was brought to light by a fellow student of mine during a lecture he gave at our ten-year reunion.

Jerry was the best of us. He gave up a prestigious residency at Massachusetts General Hospital to work as a family practitioner in the poorest county of North Carolina and was paid by the pooled funds of numerous tobacco sharecroppers. His meager compensation was supplemented by nineteen sweaters knit by his patients for his firstborn child. Seeing patients out of a refurbished one-room Baptist church many miles from paved roads or even x-ray equipment, Jerry was an adopter of evidence-based medicine much earlier than those of us practicing in large medical centers. As a quiz during our ten-year reunion, he asked our classmates to choose the single best test they might use to diagnose strep throat in a young patient coming into the office. The most common test most of us selected would have cost Jerry's patient the equivalent of one month's salary. Sensing his responsibility to be judicious in ordering tests that could destroy a family's ability to afford basic food and clothing, Jerry was forced to use every clinical skill and intuition he had absorbed as a student to find his way around those tests, and more often than not the result was sufficient and effective. He was among the first of us to use an evidence-based medical approach.

Technology can certainly be valuable in discovering asymptomatic disease, especially when dealing with commonly targeted syndromes. Yet even widely used screening tests (mammography, PSA for prostate cancer, treadmill testing, and so on) have come under scrutiny for two reasons: cost and false-positive results. Technology improves sensitivity, but human oversight increases its specificity. Together they form a powerful tool. Abandon the history or physical examination, and the system exposes the patient to false diagnosis.

CHAPTER 6

THE BODY OF INFORMATION: WHEN ANATOMY IS GROSS

Some of us fidgeted, some picked distractedly at their clothing, others unwittingly displayed facial tics suppressed since childhood, and all found it difficult to remain still. We shuffled fitfully near the entrance to the room, as if balancing on a chaotic flow of electrons beneath our feet. The high-pitched twitter of small talk was interrupted by an occasional percussion of knuckles cracking. Despite a few cocky comments piercing the silence, the air in the anteroom sizzled with electricity, betraying the universal nervousness preceding our first gross anatomy class.

The Organ Recital

By the time I walked into the lab, the all-too-familiar pungent waft of formaldehyde had already begun to burn my eyes and insult my nasal passages. There, ceremoniously draped like ancient Egyptian mummies being prepared for their eternal royal journey, lay twenty-four silent bodies—one for every two students. We crept quietly into the room, hushed, praying not to wake anyone and wary of the slightest possible twitch rippling from underneath the sheets, perhaps the result of having watched too many horror movies. Our thoughts were a tangle—some sensing the rush of finally leaping the chasm from dissecting frogs to studying humans, others taking their place as the rightful heirs of a

15th-century da Vinci or a 16th-century Vesalius, eager to reenact their ghoulish grave-robbing exploits.

There were jokes, yes, and there always will be, especially when such a displacement reaction seems to offer the only available emotional escape. This was, after all, a critical rite of passage, and most students had no idea how to center their thoughts, how to calm their self-doubt, how to express fright or flight.

A few students capriciously constructed makeshift hats with a flat cardboard visor that balanced a broad white candle like those used to light the gravesites and anatomy theaters of the 15th century, briefly dousing the room's overhead lighting to recreate the somber, morbid mood. Others boasted of a plan to abscond with a few leftover loops of bowel they hoped to hang casually from their lab coat pocket while strolling through the undergraduate library—a scheme as obnoxious as it was unrealistic. I learned about a trio who had strung a thin wire from outside the room to a male cadaver's penis, which when pulled would simulate an erection whenever a female student walked by. At another medical school, a colleague revealed that two students placed a frozen hotdog near the cadaver's penis. These students were appropriately expelled from school the next day. (Evidently, neither maturity nor originality had been a prerequisite for acceptance to the class.)

But within the first hour of disrespect, a group meeting was convened to discuss the solemnity of the moment, to facilitate the expression of fears and misgivings, and to reinforce belated gratitude toward those patients and their families who had donated their precious final gift. At first some students branded their cadaver with an amusing name, but such frivolity was soon abandoned as the actual name of each donor and a brief medical history were read aloud and honored. Giving recognition to a life well lived while peeling away the layers of the body's hidden secrets sobered the entire class. Much could be learned from our *Gray's Anatomy* tome, but even this well-worn guide was a poor substitute for flesh and the haptic response that real muscle can provide for the dissector.

The cadavers were covered with a series of damp white cloths, each roughly 24 inches by 12 inches and soaked in preservatives. In part, these protected the tissues from drying out from prolonged exposure to the air, but they also blunted the initial recoil expected of new students who had never seen a dead body. It was hard to appreciate, even a bit surreal; one day a student was putting the final touches on an English paper, and the next day she was holding someone's lung in her hand.

We removed only one cloth at a time, beginning with the one covering the armpit. Recognized as the least emotionally charged area of the body to study, the armpit allowed students time to settle into an intellectual process that required focus and intense visual memory.

I experienced a moment of absence, remembering walking on the boardwalk in Far Rockaway, New York, when I was five years old, holding my grandfather's hand and searching with him for the world's best cherry blintz. His thick fingers and warm palm dwarfed my entire hand with gentle reassurance. His nickel was always available to buy me an orange popsicle. His motionless figure could have replaced any one of the bodies lying on the metal table in front of me. Today, however, something was different, dispassionate, unreal. Our cadaver had a cool, rubbery skin tone that addled the senses and detached us from any emotional relationship, any connection of this body with those of our deceased loved ones.

As one might anticipate, the final area of dissection was the face, a region many found profoundly disturbing even weeks after having been desensitized by the rest of the body. I doubt there is a profession that launches a comparable assault on the raw nerves of its fledgling acolytes. I was told by a colleague who attended Louisiana State University that his medical school typically lost two to four students in each class during the anatomy laboratory. Anticipating this attrition, they kept a short waitlist from which to replace the dropouts during the first few weeks.

The visceral reactions from those early days of gross anatomy seem to have burned themselves into the memories of every doctor I know. Every colleague I spoke with remembers how the grease and formaldehyde insinuated themselves into everything we wore and everything we touched. Others remarked ruefully on the absence of airconditioning in the anatomy labs. Another student's table of dissectors considered themselves lucky, learning their cadaver was a man in his mid-forties with excellent anatomical structure. But before long, the macabre nature of his premature demise became evident when they exposed his assassin, the large wedge of an orange lodged in his larynx.

One former student confessed that the pressures of time demanded he acquire a special skill: dissecting with his right hand while eating a sandwich with his left. Another admitted nearly "blowing" his lunch on the first day while watching a wide-screen video demonstration on how to make the first huge incision to dissect a hip. In stark contrast to what they had experienced in their undergraduate courses, most students, humbled by the sheer complexity of the human body, admitted having to face the awful realization that they would never be able to learn everything.

In the anatomy arena at our school, innovative technology was put to good use. Large specialized slicers (called bioptomes) were developed to cut one-nanometer slivers of an entire body or of a frozen brain, photographing each slice and then constructing a video. If a student wanted to review her lesson without going back into the lab, she could visually "travel" through the body/brain while sitting at a study carrel. Three-dimensional spatial relationships, so often a source of confusion and agony for students of neuroanatomy, were facilitated, dramatically accelerating learning. The typical one to two years of gross anatomy was thereby truncated to three months—and the six months of neuroanatomy collapsed into six weeks. In my school's case, the salvaged time was devoted to introducing a research project and thesis—one of only three such required programs, along with those at Case Western Reserve and Yale, in the country.

CHAPTER 7

A RAT'S TALE

THE FOUNDING FACULTY OF MY MEDICAL SCHOOL believed strongly in developing a curriculum that went beyond teaching science; they wanted to grow scientists. Every aspect of the new curriculum was designed to interweave science with practice, research with clinical medicine. At our ten-year reunion, nearly 50 percent of our class still enjoyed careers in fulltime research.

FROM THE LATIN *SCIENTIA*, "KNOWLEDGE"

ASIDE FROM PERPETUATING the time-honored mandate to memorize scads of biochemistry formulas and reactions, the faculty devised a project in which pairs of students would be assigned a unique test tube half-filled with a brown gruel of unknown origin. The contents of the test tube were the only sample we would get; there would be no refills. Each set of partners was given six weeks to identify, isolate, and purify a specific enzyme from their test tube—a process that had never been recorded in the medical literature up to that time, so that no student could go to the library to learn how to accomplish this feat, and each pair of students was required to publish their methods and findings. For the teams comprising humanities majors, former history professors, or even math PhDs, this trial by fire was nothing short of terrifying. Some depleted their samples, others lost their nearly purified enzyme after clumsily smashing their Sephadex columns, the three-foot long glass tubes filled with fluid and a sand-like substance used to help separate the enzyme from other contaminants. The process was designed to replicate the feeling of the isolated investigator of the early 20th century on his journey into the unknown. Except, of course, the lives of the world did not hang in the balance as it did during the Spanish influenza. The race against time was not even for a grade; it was merely a matter of pride.

Appreciating that nature guards her secrets jealously, we learned to pay special attention to what did not work; the truth was more often hidden in the error, the overlooked departure from the expected, the outlier. No more rigorous a lesson was taught to us than by the chair of pathology, Dr. Averill Liebow. Short and thick yet commanding, and never at a loss for words, he orated with an 18th-century British eloquence. Liebow had brought with him most of the pathology department from Yale, where he had been chair. How well I remember the first words he uttered to the class during the first morning of school, when a panel of department chairs introduced themselves. The new chair of radiology, who came from the National Institutes of Health, gave an overview of his area of discipline and then, with a sarcastic smile and twinkle in his eye, announced, "And now it is my great honor to introduce to you Dr. Averill Liebow, Chair of Pathology... for whatever that field is worth."

Liebow's confident rejoinder: "I have always believed that substance is more important than shadow."

Echoing the mantra of the famous 19th-century French physician Claude Bernard, "Science teaches us to doubt," Liebow approached the microscope with the wariness and mindset that typified the objective scientist. In addition to partaking in his lectures, we spent hours trying to identify his unlabeled histology teaching slides.

Liebow acknowledged that when first looking at a tissue specimen under the microscope, he would invariably be struck with an obvious diagnosis. His teaching goal, however, was to set this inclination aside and to try to make the case for all the alternative pathologies it could possibly represent, to prove his first intuition wrong. If the characteristics of all the others could not be supported, his first conclusion was most likely to be the right one. Quoting Bernard once more, he reminded us that "It is what we know already that often prevents us from learning." Our preconceptions, we were to learn, can bias our thinking and impede progress.

Just to test the waters, one capricious student made a histology slide of a baby alligator's lung. He had purchased the neonate from a local pet store, but it had looked sluggish from the start and survived for only a few weeks. He handed the slide to Dr. Liebow:

"Sir, I'm having a little trouble identifying what disease this represents. Could you give me your opinion?" he asked with a retrograde wink.

Liebow bent over the scope, mulling over the options. Wearing a collective smirk, the students who were in on the plot gathered behind the professor in anticipation.

Scratching the back of his neck in feigned befuddlement, Liebow replied, "I really have no idea from what kind of pneumonia this poor reptile was suffering." No one in our class could have expected that an expert in human pathology would recognize non-mammalian lung tissue, but neither were they yet aware that Dr. Liebow was the world's foremost lung pathologist—the first to discover and classify a new category of diseases called interstitial pneumonias—and had been recently honored by the NIH as Pathologist of the Decade. A wiser smart aleck might at least have chosen tissue from a less familiar organ.

Of course, most students entered school to become caregivers, but all agreed to invest at least 30 percent of their time in developing and publishing a science project somewhat akin to a PhD research thesis. Each built an advisory team that not only guided him through the project but also supported the submission of the resulting work to a nationally recognized journal. Moreover, the team coached the candidate in preparation for the public defense of his dissertation before a panel of experts in the field.

The span of interests in science projects reflected both the broad background of our student class as well as their growing interest in highly specific fields of medicine. One of my roommates, who later became a neonatologist, studied a rare genetic disorder, I-cell disease. Another roommate investigated the difference in a muscle enzyme between West Coast and East Coast lobster tails, ensuring an endless supply of seafood delicacies and a smooth, unchallenging path to becoming an ER doctor. The third nurtured an early interest in SIDS (sudden infant death syndrome), a field he has come to dominate as professor of pediatric pulmonary disease at Children's Hospital Los Angeles.

THE DISCOVERY CHANNEL: OF ENZYMES AND EXPERIMENTS

SOMEHOW, WHEN MY ADVISOR (and the man who was to become my mentor for the next twenty years) suggested I study cardiac enzymes, I never imagined I would be working so intimately with rats. I am not referring to the cute little creatures some animal lover might enjoy as a pet; I'm talking about the one-kilogram aging, vicious, yellowed-toothed male rats. These malevolent rodents had already endured several lab experiments; scarred, injected, and irradiated, they were now embarking on their final journey... and they sensed it.

I worked in a makeshift lab on a bluff overlooking the shores of Del Mar near the grounds of the new Salk Institute. My first assignment was to comb the library over a six-week period for the world's literature on the CPK enzyme. I was asked to choose one method (polyacrylamide gel electrophoresis) that had successfully isolated the enzyme from the rat's heart tissue and start my project by simply reproducing the data from a groundbreaking index article. I selected a definitive paper published by an eminent researcher at a world-class research institution. Once that was accomplished, I planned to determine if I could identify this same enzyme in a blood sample taken from a lab animal following a heart attack—a marker that would subsequently be used to detect and quantify very early heart damage in humans.

For more than a year, I struggled in vain to replicate the methods in the paper described by the renowned senior scientist. "One key to science is that work be reproducible," wrote John M. Barry, describing the new science of medicine in his book *The Great Influenza*. "Someone in another laboratory doing the same experiment will get the same result. The result then is reliable enough that someone else can build upon it. The most damning condemnation is to dismiss a finding as 'not reproducible.'"

I became obsessed with this experiment: the pH of the renowned researcher's solutions, the diameter of the Tygon tubing he used, and the method of enzyme separation he described. In short, I took every single detail he listed in the Methods and Materials section of his paper to bed with me every night and on most weekends, but to no avail. Nothing I did seemed to work as he had written, which was hugely frustrating. When it came time for me to quantify the enzyme that I was supposed to identify by staining it with a special preparation, I got nothing; no stained enzyme was ever visible. My advisor just kept sending me back to the lab to let me try to work through the minutia, hoping I would eventually discover where my laboratory setup deviated from what had been published.

I poured hundreds of failed experiments down the drain over the next fourteen months. Having hit the proverbial wall and in a fit of temporary insanity, I picked up the telephone and called the lead author of the study at the research mecca. As a mere sophomore, I certainly had no realistic expectation of speaking with this respected investigator, but to my amazement, he answered the call himself. So close was I to the methodology of his paper, so familiar with every trivial nuance and detail, that within seconds of our conversation I recognized, stunned, that he had never performed the experiment!

The phone receiver almost fell out of my hand. I went momentarily numb, revived, and then raced into my advisor's office, breathless and a little wild-eyed. No wonder I had been unsuccessful; the paper was a sham!

"Burt," I yelled. "That guy at the institute dry-labbed the experiment!"

"I know," he exclaimed calmly, not even pausing to look up from his desk.

I must admit it took a few seconds for it all to penetrate. I barely had time to reimagine the hundreds of sleepless nights of discouragement and anguish, of worry that my project was going nowhere, that I would never complete my task, that I was an utter failure as an enzymologist. Dazed at first, I marched back to the lab and within thirty minutes set up the simple experiment that answered the pivotal, gnawing question. I lined up a series of small vials with one different ingredient missing in each vial. Then I added the stain to see which vial failed to take up the stain. I flew back into my advisor's office.

"Burt!" I announced. "Polyacrylamide gel destroys my enzyme." This gel was the method I was using to separate my enzyme from the tissue—the one described in the published article.

"I know," he said, a faint smile now peeking through the attention he still pretended to lavish on his desk papers.

Saying nothing, I turned and walked slowly away. A year of my life had been squandered. I was dumbfounded, even angry, that my advisor had known all along that the study was erroneous, impossible, a fraud, and yet had not helped me through the straits. Wasn't that his job? Isn't that what an advisor is supposed to do?

Perusing the literature, I uncovered a simple alternative method of separating enzyme proteins. Working furiously over the next few months, I employed the technique that would lead to my discovery of a new molecular subunit of CPK enzyme and the subject of my thesis as well as three subsequent papers. It was only then, when I came up for air, that I understood my advisor's faint smile that day, his signal that I had transitioned from student to scientist. This is a transformative journey that no one can make on someone else's behalf, one that can neither be taught in a lecture hall nor memorized from a book.

Creatures Furry, Fast, and Furious

I SHOULD MENTION AT THIS JUNCTURE that throughout these experiments, the rats were not exactly models of cooperation. Somebody, and God only knows who, made the decision that young scientists should become familiar with handling lab animals without the use of protective gloves. The technique of grabbing a rat's tail with my fifth finger, and then rapidly marching up the animal's back and tightly securing the skin behind the neck was designed to avoid being bitten. I was at first too easily convinced of the theoretical brilliance behind this approach, until I realized that this was not these rats' first rodeo. I triumphed most of the time, but I do have a few scars to prove my underestimation of the strength of a large male rat's neck muscles.

Lab animals were housed in the basement of a research institute in small tile-walled rooms lined with deep stainless-steel drawers, each containing up to eight rats. (I read somewhere that a collection of rats is aptly referred to as "a mischief.") This particular mischief of fresh cellmates had arrived only the day before, and I was quite sure they sensed my palpitations as I gingerly opened one of those drawers to peek inside. The sound judgment my parents had tried to instill in me screamed that what I was about to do was not a good idea. All eight of those creatures, positively Olympian in stature, stood up on their hind legs and bared their brownish incisors at my sweaty, naked hand, which darted in and out of the bin as, terrorized, I tried to grab hold of one.

After nearly an hour of panic and multiple failed incursions, I finally managed to extricate one rat from the bin by his tail, but his powerful front paws latched on to the front rim of the drawer and pulled it crashing to the floor. Seven maniacal—and likely equally terrified—rats then scattered to the four corners of the room, as I mindlessly dropped the one I already had kidnapped while I raced to close the door to the room, lest they escape to who knows where. So that I now found myself locked in a small basement room with eight frenzied monsters scurrying in all directions. Whenever I tried to corner one he would rear up and, in a final attempt to repel my advances, run up my pant leg in attack mode. They made a growling noise designed, I am sure, to intimidate their foe, and believe me, that strategy worked well for quite some time. I seriously considered the option of just quietly tiptoeing out, closing the door behind me, and allowing someone else to discover the jailbreak. One cannot always fully explain a "mischief"!

But instead, after an exhausting hour of crazed thrust and parry, I eventually tossed one rat at a time against the wall, stunning them long enough to deposit all eight back into the bin without having my hand devoured. Their muscle enzyme levels now sky-high (and doubtless mine as well), any results I reported in my study would be spurious. With perhaps the first but certainly not the last experiment gone awry, I ultimately learned to cull the rats with greater calm, and they responded by politely donating their bodies with more acquiescence.

I fear this next piece will bother more than a few readers, and I admit that it took some time for me to overcome my own reluctance to participate in the study. Hoping that the potential benefit to the future treatment of patients was worth the pursuit (a conclusion that turned out to be absolutely correct), I managed to put my initial objections aside, even when my resolve was seriously shaken. The success of the rat model dictated a move to a larger animal model—the rabbit. When the three- and five-year-old sons of one research fellow from Norway with whom I was working poked their heads into the lab unannounced one day, delighted that their daddy and I were "helping the bunnies," it was an unnerving reminder that we were experimenting on Thumper, Bugs, Peter Cottontail, and the White Rabbit.

To study certain enzymes in a still-beating heart, I needed to use lab animals of larger caliber. The experimental model called for the surgical removal of a rabbit's beating heart followed by its attachment to a tube that could perfuse oxygenated fluids through the aorta (and coronary arteries) for several hours. Under these controlled conditions, certain biochemical functions could be studied as I tried to mimic the effects of a heart attack. With the proper fluids, the heart would continue to beat outside the body for hours. Measuring the heart's expenditure of energy meant trying to keep the volume of the left ventricle (the main pumping chamber of the heart) uniform—in other words, asking the heart to contract, but always to the same degree and to the exact internal dimension, a way to control as many variables as possible. After attempting several design options that failed due to poor durability, I found the most effective solution involved cutting off the very tip of a condom, tying it to a piece of rigid tubing, and placing the small inflated "balloon" into the cavity of the left ventricle. That way, the ventricle's size remained constant.

Each day for nearly an entire summer, I sauntered into the same pharmacy in La Jolla and carelessly asked the eighty-year-old white-haired pharmacist if I could purchase up to a dozen condoms. In those days, the conservative town was openly suspicious of the intrusion of a new "radical" university populace, so one could appreciate his rationale for guarding the prophylactics in the display case behind the counter. Day after day, the elderly pharmacist stoically complied with my request. After many weeks, however, I once again entered the pharmacy trying to project my supply needs for an upcoming four-day weekend of work. Absorbed and oblivious to how this must have sounded, I calculated out loud.

"Let me see.... I'm looking at a four-day vacation, and I do have almost the whole day."

The old man, pomade plastering his hair neatly down the middle, his frail frame meticulously packaged into a heavily starched white coat, fixated on me like a laser. His eyebrows accordioned in the middle, forming an eave that hung over his eyes, now a deeper blue against his ashen face as he leaned forward for my instructions.

"You'd better give me a gross," I concluded, satisfied with my estimates. The old man, startled, audibly sucked in a full breath, and then exhaled slowly in resignation.

Carefully counting out the twelve-dozen prophylactics, he whispered, "Anything you say, Superman."

I don't think I ever explained to the poor fellow that his awe was completely unfounded. Science was stimulating, all right, but not quite the way my little pharmacist imagined.

CHAPTER 8

TRANSLATING LIFE THROUGH THE LENS OF SCIENCE

Archimedes's "Eureka" moment, Bell's "Watson, come here," and similar epiphanies that headline chapters in the history of science are obviously unique and rare, as were any of the capstones built on a foundation of critical thinking. Most scientists, however, including those who witness sudden scientific revelation, are cultivated slowly, grown tall by their exposure to the elements and molded by experience. Our biostatistics professor once illustrated to our class an example of how pseudoscientists draw erroneous conclusions by identifying facts that appear to correlate but are in fact random.

In 1945 post-war Germany, the birth rate fell to its lowest level in decades (and since). During that same period, the German equivalent of the Audubon Society described a significant decline in the sighting of storks in their country. The conclusion, of course, was that storks deliver babies.

So many cause-and-effect relationships are incorrectly presumed when two facts appear to agree until defrocked by critical analysis. As a budding scientist, I decided I must practice examining the world around me with the same scientific eye that I used in the lab.

New Vistas from Old Worlds

I spent a portion of my sophomore year in London, taking my pediatrics rotations at Guy's Hospital, extra rounds at Great Ormand Street (of *Peter*

Pan fame), and neurology at the renowned neurological institute at Queen's Square. These institutions were swollen with medical history. I wandered the halls on the eponymous wards of both Addison and Hodgkin—denizens of Guy's Hospital's prior staff. Dr. Philip Evans, chief of pediatrics, took me on a personal tour of the Gordon Museum of Pathology, the largest medical museum in the UK. This remarkable facility is home to thousands of preserved specimens, the first examples of diseases whose names I had only just memorized. Next he marched me to the roof of the hospital to point out the house in which Charles Dickens was born.

The interior hall entrance to the neurological institute rose several stories, the walls emblazoned with a medical dictionary of personalities. Large brass plaques lined the stone surfaces, a standing ovation to honor the syndromes that filled every complete neurology textbook, acknowledging Queen's Square as the birth mother of these great names. The neurologists who trained here were among the best bedside clinicians in the world. A team (including my famous attending, Dr. Roger Bannister, known for his medical skills almost as much as for having broken the world record for running the first four-minute mile) routinely toured the city, examining every patient in psychiatric hospitals each year and ferreting out those with subtle organic diseases who presented as having purely psychiatric problems. The medical team's expertise at physical examination was unparalleled. But typically, the specialist with the greatest grasp of differential diagnosis, I was to learn, was the radiologist.

Possibly to conserve healthcare funds but more likely as a sincere mental callisthenic, radiologists were used as consultants, not employees who blindly carried out orders. Ward physicians did not reflexively prescribe a battery of x-rays and scans that the radiology department then automatically obliged. Instead, after presenting the patient's history and physical findings, the attending physician conferred with the radiologist to ascertain the *single* best test to confirm the diagnosis. These consultations saved money and were effective learning experiences for generalists. My classmate Jerry, practicing in the far reaches of rural North Carolina, as well as the healthcare budget, would have approved.

When Science Charts the Stars

ONCE MY STUDY PROGRAMS were complete and with a few free weeks ahead, I allowed the wind and serendipity to cast me around Europe. So much of my life leading to medical school had been prescribed that I now chose to opt for some planned spontaneity. I traveled without reservations, maps, or guidebook, in an experiment with myself.

After a superficial discussion with a group of Americans I had just met at a café in Basel, Switzerland, I was easily convinced to follow them for a few days into the mountains. At their recommendation, I found myself checking into a small inn called the Club Vagabond atop an isolated hill a few miles from the small alpine town of Leysin. Remote and free of tourism, the area boasted nothing more exotic than a pleasant view of some hills sparsely decorated with greenery, but an environment ideal for consuming novels. Watching the shadows wend their way from left to right provided a welcome recess from the hectic pace of school and concentration on matters of science.

The inn was populated by a cross section of students, writers, "spiritualists," and even a small coterie of edgy, tattooed clientele representing the most peripheral spectrum of the human species. While admiring the span of the late-night Milky Way one evening, I met two thirty-something astrologers who had been orbiting the inn for the past week and who were busy mapping planetary movements they believed influenced our future. We engaged in some spirited discourse—a young scientist and two pseudoscientists—and it was not long before an impasse was reached and a gauntlet thrown down. I had expressed enough disbelief in astrology to confront the very core of their raison d'être.

"Do you happen to know the exact time of your birth *within four minutes?*" they inquired suspiciously.

Eyes rolling, I admitted that I did.

"Doesn't everybody?" I responded casually, barely concealing a hint of snarkiness.

Rising to the challenge, they proposed to chart my detailed horoscope (an effort that took them nearly forty-eight hours to complete), promising to predict my entire life story. I gave them the information they sought, and they huddled in their room for the next two days, absorbed in their calculations. Emerging with astrological graphs in hand, constellations packaged, and my sun and moon-rising trajectories charted, they met me with confidence on the front lawn. The valley was their sole witness.

To my absolute astonishment, I had to confess that their predictions were spot on! Triumphant and grinning from dreadlock to dreadlock when I acknowledged how precise and specific their findings were, they shared high fives all around. The most stunning aspect of this entire experience, however, was that I had purposely given them the wrong birth date! By exposing my deceit to them, I had no intention to embarrass or ridicule, simply to inform. Science, you see, requires a control group to be conclusive. Science is about knowing, measuring, observing, and rethinking one's conclusions. I slipped out of the inn early the next morning, persona non grata but condescendingly scientific.

Probing the Heart of the Studies

FLEXING MY NEWLY FORMED SCIENCE MUSCLES, I continued wandering Europe for the next few weeks, occasionally dropping in at local medical libraries to keep up with the latest discoveries and practice "seeing through" any faulty methodology that still pervaded a few less credible journals. The recent groundswell in evidence-based medical literature demanded that, going forward, we relegate noncritical thinking to the dustbins of scientific history.

Because biological systems introduce so many complex variables, apparently trivial differences in study design can render a journal article and its hypothesis either positive or negative. For its nearly twenty years under the editorial guidance of Dr. Arnold Relman, the eminent *New England Journal of Medicine* would publish back-to-back articles from two different institutions describing seemingly identical study designs yet offering opposing results. Baffling as it was to medical students and other naive readers, Dr. Relman always managed to call upon a luminary in the field to provide an editorial in the same issue elucidating how these controversies could coexist.

In the field of cardiology, one example comes to mind. Waged over decades, the dispute involved whether anticoagulants (blood thinners) should be used to improve survival in patients with heart attacks. Data accumulated from seemingly similar patient cohorts and using complementary methods appeared to show contradicting results. One prominent group of researchers claimed giving blood thinners was valuable, and another equally prestigious group argued against it. Both sides supported their positions with convincing hypotheses, statistics, and graphs. Before long, studies were being published from institutions around the world aligning themselves with one camp or the other. Those who understood how real science should be used to drive vital medical practice sought clarity in the editorial that summarized and justified how both conclusions were correct.

First, it was necessary to appreciate the fact that heart attacks are acute events that evolve over time. Much like a city in which a volcano had erupted, a central area of complete destruction could be seen surrounded by a zone of partial damage—some buildings flattened, some ready to collapse, others still intact. So too a heart attack first creates a dense epicenter of heart muscle damage that begins to spread outward like a moving wall of lava over the next twenty-four hours. Peripheral heart tissue, which is sick, hangs in the balance and may either survive or succumb, depending on the metabolic health of its environment.

The damage can be quantified by measuring the area under a curve produced by a rise in heart tissue enzymes that leak into the bloodstream, reflecting dying muscle. From that curve we can observe and calculate precisely how much damage was done. If, however, one traced that completed enzyme curve backward, statisticians found they could predict and reproduce the entire curve (and the damage that was going to take place) after only five hours. So any therapeutic intervention begun at the five-hour mark that changed the curve would allow a measure of predicted damage vs. observed damage. Now the table was set to provide a test that could determine the efficacy of a whole variety of therapies ... including blood thinners.

The key difference in the studies of anticoagulants resulted from how soon they could be administered. If anticoagulants were given early, the clot that closed the coronary artery producing the heart attack could be partially dissolved, allowing muscle-nourishing blood flow to save tissue that would otherwise have died. Administered too late, when small arteries in the central area of damage had already become fragile, the dissolution of a clot could cause small arteries to explode and bleed into the wall of the heart muscle, creating further destruction. This might be analogous to the benefit of opening a clogged pipeline with a Roto-Rooter machine vs. the detriment of exposing a weakened pipe to high water pressure, resulting in a massive leak.

Having learned to dissect Methods and Materials from my own research in medical school, I learned to tweeze apart these differences and better understand as a budding scientist how to approach treatment for my future patients. Critical analysis of the "smaller" details often held the answers to apparent discrepancies in publications. Drilling down on these points, often easily overlooked, became the central measure of the good future physician.

Clinical Teaching and Meaningful Research: Is There Room for Both?

Although many students currently attending my former school who are interested in research choose to pursue a combined MD-PhD degree similar to the program I was part of, the edict that all students must be involved in an in-depth research experience is no longer in force. One could argue that this decision is both unfortunate and rational. All practicing physicians could certainly benefit from conceiving and honing a hypothesis, refining an experimental model, massaging and analyzing the data, and confronting the rigorous (and often contentious) public defense of his research. As he applies the burdens of proof to his own project, he learns to demand the same specificity from the medical literature he later scrutinizes.

Conversely, the prolonged years of training required for many specialties has become unsustainable. For those candidates whose primary intent is direct patient care, the expenditure of additional time on research becomes a luxury. For example, a neurosurgery resident begins her training as a general surgeon and has completed her prerequisites seven years after a four-year medical school curriculum. After medical school, cardiology specialization entails a three-year residency in internal medicine, followed by three to four years of fellowship (depending on whether a year of research is required), and additional years for further subspecialty training in electrophysiology, interventional cardiology, or transplant medicine. Graduates complete their studies already in their mid-thirties and are often profoundly in debt.

Current statistics disclose that eight out of ten medical students assume tuition debt averaging $250,000 or more, while 18 percent of them borrow more than $300,000. Despite the significant six-figure salary for a young physician (at the low end, pediatricians earn about $180,00 a year compared with surgeons, whose annual earnings average $255,000), the median time to repay the debt exceeds thirteen years.

So while training programs should ideally weave bench science into their curricula, this may not always be practical, especially when highly skilled procedures must be taught. Should every physician be trained to be a generalist before becoming a specialist? We are often reminded of the tongue-in-cheek commentary "Specialists are physicians who learn more and more about less and less until they know everything about nothing; generalists are physicians who learn less and less about more and more until they know nothing about everything."

Clearly, doctors face the enormous challenge (and the losing race) between the rapidity with which medical science expands vs. the limited time available for its mastery. Thus, the thirty-something specialist emerges from decades of training only to finally begin payment of her substantial loans. She encounters declining reimbursements, demands by her patients to constantly update access to costly specialty equipment, and other massive overhead expenses including the purchase of electronic medical records. Competition with expanding hospital outpatient services becomes untenable, making independence from the hospital network increasingly difficult. These pressures may subtly, subconsciously favor the young doctor's decisions to order more expensive, more lucrative testing.

Factoring in these considerations, it is no surprise there is so little time for anything more than a dabbling of research in medical school curricula for students bent on becoming clinicians. And more often, future scientists find the time spent on the broader requirements of medical school simply detracts from the angular bench research in which they hope to engage. There exists, of course, a gifted group of graduates who manage to juggle a clinical medical practice with clinical research, but they are typically affiliated with a teaching institution and have the luxury of extensive support from house staff.

CHAPTER 9

THE SNAKE, THE HORNED TOAD, AND THE IGUANA

A BATTALION OF RABBITS, scampering across the dusty road and narrowly evading our tires, were made skittish by the unfamiliar din of our motorized caravan. A choir of coyotes yowled in disappointment that their efforts in marking their territory had been unsuccessful in warding off trespassers.

We arrived at the new graduate student apartments built into the sparsely populated, once-pristine hills of University City, north of San Diego and near La Jolla. To be honest, it all looked a little abandoned. Ours were the only three cars in the parking lot, since our classes began weeks before those of any other graduate schools. My three roommates and I cracked open the front door and peered inside. The smell of drying paint and virgin carpet intimated that we were the apartment complex's earliest inhabitants, but evidently that was not altogether true, because in the middle of the living room floor basked a rather large, intimidating black snake. To a city boy like me, anything that slithered and looked remotely ominous had to be a rattler or a mamba. Although the serpent did not express his alarm, I opted to call the campus police.

Our savior, the officer, was an eighteen-year-old freshman wearing a veneer of facial acne and a heavily starched uniform that failed to dominate his layers of baby fat. He stole into the room cautiously, almost on tiptoe, drawing his shiny handgun for what must have been its debut, and prepared to discharge it ... INDOORS! He was wisely halted by one of my roommates, who instead retrieved a tire iron from the trunk of his recently acquired Renault jalopy, bravely slew the reptile, and threw it out the kitchen window. I was relieved that no bullet holes had blemished our new carpet and grateful no ricochets had prematurely ended anyone's career.

A year later, when we decided to rent a four-bedroom house together, we were inspired to construct a little memorial to our reptile squatter, who'd paid the ultimate price in the wilderness of University City. My roommate built a six-foot-long terrarium equipped with heating lamps and a water feature in which to house three new pets. Each was fondly named after one of the Giants: Averill, the horned toad, named after the chief of pathology (you have already met his namesake); Marshall, the iguana, named after the chief of surgery; and Eugene, the eleven-foot anaconda, after the chief of medicine. Between our wildlife trio and our student quartet, we lived contently in our Mission Beach habitat, but we rattled many of our conservative neighbors, unaccustomed as they were to this encroachment on suburbia. Peering over the backyard fence, some would shyly inquire if something "radical" was going on in there? Truly, they needed to worry only about our pets' escaping when we brought them out during toga parties, and even then, our guests' Age of Aquarius costumes more often provoked the neighbors' anxiety than did the cold-blooded fauna.

We fed the anaconda secondhand lab mice, all of whom had previously been involved in a variety of experiments and a few of whom might still have been marginally radioactive. Well, for whatever reason, this diet did not seem to agree with Eugene, who true to his namesake became exceedingly dyspeptic and turned a bit aggressive. After biting one of my housemates on the shoulder while his cage was being cleaned, Eugene was ultimately banished from the terrarium and donated to a grateful San Diego Zoo.

Down by the Liverside

WHILE THIS STORY HAD LITTLE TO DO directly with the training program, it was a reminder of how we integrated daily life with our ward experience. Our first surgical rotation was with Marshall, the chief of surgery and first-cousin-once-removed to our iguana. Marshall had pioneered a surgical treatment for end-stage liver disease called a portacaval shunt, which involved making a large abdominal incision and connecting the portal vein (supplying 75 percent of the blood to the liver) to the inferior vena cava (the large vein returning blood from the lower half of the body). The surgery was designed to decrease liver pressure that could cause life-threatening bleeding. Typically, this grueling, six-hour operation called for a medical student continuously pulling with all his might to retract a gigantic, swollen liver with a Deaver, akin to a short-handled garden hoe. Purported to be a learning experience, this activity was in reality an opportunity to spend half a day admiring the back of Marshall's neck—or "making black mole rounds," a term we coined in tribute to his benign lesion, which we came to know intimately. The boredom was excruciating, but trivial compared with the stiffness and pain in one's arms, shoulders, and back. This time I had the dubious honor of performing such a stand-up job (literally) that it merited a positive nod of recognition. Just then and almost before we had time to remove our surgical gloves, a second patient hit the ER with acute liver failure. Marshall told me to scrub in for the second case—a compliment that lasted twelve hours. I never considered declining the offer, nor would have any of my classmates. Such were the times. That evening I fell asleep standing up in the bathroom with my head propped against the mirror.

In today's medical schools, this arduous stint would likely never take place, and perhaps any objection I considered raising back then might have resulted in only a tiny improvement in the training process. The indelibility of the lesson, however, was unrelated to acquiring a deeper scholarly understanding of liver pathology; it had more to do with an appreciation of the tenacity and focus of a surgeon. That day there was no second shift, no tag team to take over mid-operation. Marshall was, at that time, possibly the only person in the world able to perform this operation, the only one who also devoted *his* twelve solid hours to saving two lives. There was no other choice, no rationalization, no compromise. I was a small, expendable observer in the OR, but I witnessed something profound about dedication. Had I opted to merely read the chart the next day rather than feel the ache in my arms, I would never have known the entire story. Some vital part of the lesson would have lost its heft, become less vivid, faded with time. Years later, the lesson would have been forgotten, and perhaps Marshall's drive might not have inspired a similar dedication in my future practice.

STRESS FRACTURES: THE PSYCHE UNDER FIRE

STANDING IN THE BACK ROW of the OR had its advantages, since you were less likely to get into trouble there. One of my roommates found this lesson out the hard way during his freshman year. His rather aggressive surgery professor had gained national approbation when he removed a live grenade from a soldier's abdomen during the Vietnam War, and even though he'd performed the delicate surgery partially buffered by some bales of hay, his hands were obviously exposed to the danger of a sudden explosion. A year later, in the middle of a routine chest operation, the surgeon invited my roommate, Tom, to come get a better view. As Tom leaned forward hesitantly to examine the anatomy, his glasses fell into the chest cavity (calling to mind a much later *Seinfeld* episode in which Kramer loses a Jujube in a patient's abdomen).

"Why don't you just take a dump in the chest while you're at it?" screeched the surgeon.

His was the frame of mind of more than one surgeon scarred by their service in the armed forces during that era in American history. In many a civilian operating room, however, frustrated surgeons have been known to hurl instruments and even purposely stab assistants with scalpels and skin hooks, or casually zap them with an electrocautery, more correctly used to stop small blood vessels from bleeding inside a wound. Students, often out of fear for their future letters of recommendation, usually chose to let these atrocities pass.

The abuse dished out by the Giants was certainly not limited to anger-management lapses in the OR. The wish to generate an impactful teaching moment could itself be an invitation to castigate. Some of us chose to believe that the Giants' purpose in dispensing this torture was motivated less by a sadistic impulse as it was to promote humility. One such humbling example from the early 1970s that took place at Parkland Hospital in Dallas was witnessed by a colleague.

A third-year female student was invited to stand and present her patient's case history to the chairman of the department of medicine, Dr. Don Seldin, a Giant in the field of nephrology. She, like countless other students who had been put on display, was shaking uncontrollably. Halfway through her presentation, the chief abruptly interrupted her.

"What was the serum sodium level on that day?"

Caught off guard, the student stammered. She was not allowed to refer to the chart but was expected to be intimately familiar with her patient's lab data. She racked her brain in a futile attempt to recall.

"Um …" she mumbled under her breath.

"What was the serum sodium level?" the chief insisted.

"I, uh, I am not so sure …" she continued, now appearing pale and sweaty.

"What was the serum sodium?" The chief hammered away relentlessly, his voice notching up a few decibels.

With this, the student began to sway, lost consciousness, and finally collapsed on the podium floor with a thud. The chief jumped up, ran over to the girl, and leaned over her as she opened her eyes.

"I asked you, *What was the serum sodium!?*" he screamed.

Such was the power of the Giants. In one training program on the first day the students arrived to meet the chief (Anaconda, who else?), one bright young fellow introduced himself with his long, traditional

Pakistani name. The chief paused, hovered over the nervous man for a moment, pointed an index finger at him and proclaimed:

"From now on, your name is Dave." And so it was.

I was fortunate to have somehow escaped most of the arrows slung at those fellow students who had been impaled publicly, although I endured their pain vicariously. The school's trendsetting decision to launch a pass-fail grading system united us in a common cause against ignorance. Back then a few schools still employed a pyramidal system of grading: At the end of the freshman year of medical school, the bottom third of the class was sent home. As a result, the competition was fierce, impeding rather than accelerating learning and flying in the face of the team efforts doctors depend upon in their fight against disease.

Watching my classmates writhe during an assault incentivized me to be as compulsive as possible in my own preparation. Even as a fourth-year student, when I took a one-month ear, nose, and throat surgery elective, I pregamed the rotation by going back into the anatomy theater to repeat an entire head and neck dissection to refamiliarize myself with the structures. I was bent on obviating any potential derision from the famously sarcastic department chair, who had gained recognition for having performed the tonsillectomies and tracheostomies on many Hollywood stars.

Despite my drive to be prepared for all situations in this, my last month of medical school, I was unexpectedly maneuvered into an uncomfortable corner. I was told to scrub in on a tonsillectomy on an eighteen-year-old girl. By itself, this directive seemed nothing unusual—except I had never seen a case performed, she was to be operated upon under only local anesthesia... and I was to be the surgeon!

We sat in chairs facing each other knee-to-knee, I in surgical attire and she wide awake with her mouth open. Tentatively, I began to insert the needle as I was instructed somewhere near the tonsils, when the resident standing over my shoulder casually mentioned how close the carotid artery was to the tonsils. For the first and only time during my four years of school, I began to perspire, then swayed rhythmically in a tenuous semicircle for a few seconds before passing out. Fortunately, I was caught in mid-flight by the resident and injured only my ego. Embarrassed, I eventually absolved myself from shame, concluding that medical school would not have been complete without having endured at least one such episode—merely another example of the byproduct of being placed under unreasonable stress in an impossibly foreign situation. Just as I was beginning to feel solid about my ability to handle the prospect of next month's internship, I was being taught a lesson in humility and humiliation as much as in ENT.

As you can see, there were days when the Giants walked the earth distributing intellectual magic beans, and days when the Orcs attacked those less able to defend themselves. These were times when Dr. DeBakey's surgical trainees were required to live in the cardiac surgical intensive care unit for ninety days without leaving, with meals brought to them, haircuts arranged when necessary, and sleeping quarters available but rarely occupied. Thankfully, these abusive incidents are unknown (or at least far less common) in today's programs. Partially in response to such behavior, the Accreditation Council for Graduate Medical Education paved the way to heed the plaintive voices of house staff everywhere. I will review the rationale and impact of these policies in a future chapter.

CHAPTER 10

A FEW LOOSE SCREWS

MEDICAL SCHOOL WAR STORIES are replete with the refrains of "if only" and "what if." These episodes burrow and fester under our psychic skin for decades, emerging later as either gilded triumphs or guilty tragedies and play an important role in what we come to call "our clinical experience." Sarcastically defined as the last two disasters he witnessed, a doctor's clinical experience is much more than how many operations or procedures he performed. A few select vignettes can color or stain the entirety of his career. But with the blemish comes his pledge to avoid the same mistake twice, to permit neither luck, poor judgment, misinformation, ego, nor sloth to ever interfere with success again. Always a subset of traumatic clinical experience is the *correct* decision that did not work out, because either the presentation of disease or the response to therapy was not typical. By their very nature biological systems vary, and thus they plot the coordinates of the unpredictable bell-shaped curve.

IF ONLY ...

THE FOUNDING CHIEF OF MEDICINE of my school, world-famous Dr. Braunwald (whom you may remember as "Eugene," the namesake of our anaconda), told a poignant story of his earliest days as a student, which I still remember. He was basically an observer in an outpatient clinic when a woman was to be admitted for some undisclosed illness. Her husband tagged along to provide emotional support, but while he waited to hear about his wife's disposition, he leaned over to young medical student Braunwald to mention that he had lost a small screw to his eyeglasses. He wondered if there might be a way for him to have it replaced in the interim. Anxious to be of some quasi-clinical assistance, Eugene directed him to the eye clinic and called the receptionist to make a drop-in appointment.

Upon his arrival at the clinic, the man admitted to the ophthalmologist that he had not had an eye examination in quite some time and agreed to spend a moment now. As the doctor performed the retinal exam, he saw alarming manifestations of retinal hemorrhaging often associated with severe hypertension. He confirmed that the man, while symptom free, had an alarmingly elevated blood pressure. A bit overwhelmed by the implied urgency of these circumstances, the man was whisked over to Admissions and hospitalized for further testing. His CT scan identified a huge, rare tumor of the adrenal gland (a 54-gram pheochromocytoma) which was secreting large quantities of adrenaline into his bloodstream and was responsible for his monumental blood pressure recordings.

Within a few days, the man was swept into the operating room to have this tumor excised, but in the middle of the surgery as the tumor was being removed, the patient's blood pressure plummeted, he developed a catastrophic heart rhythm disturbance, and he succumbed. Thirty years later, the chief of medicine still carried this "if only" case history in his mental pocket ... the image of an unsuspecting man who took a student's innocent advice to his grave. Even though the fateful course of this tumor's natural history would have likely been the same had it been diagnosed at a later date, the timing with Eugene's intervention was too proximate to ignore as pure circumstance. The story became a permanent part of the chief's clinical experience. Recounting this episode as a cautionary tale, the chief predicted there would be times in our own careers when we would make the right medical decision that might still end in failure.

Fowl Play

Stories about metaphorical loose screws circulate throughout all medical schools, each providing some valuable lesson that tempers the kind of doctor one becomes. One well-documented story took place in one of the "knife and gun club" hospitals serving Harvard Medical School. A homeless man wandered into the emergency room early one winter. Looking drawn and ashen, he nearly swooned, then vomited blood on the floor in front of the entire staff. He was admitted for a typical Harvard workup that lasted most of the snowy months in Boston, yet no diagnosis could be established.

Come spring, the man checked out of the hospital only to recreate this scenario each winter. Speculations ran wild with each subsequent admission. Professors and students offering exotic explanations remained puzzled by their failure to identify a cause. At last, one year as the familiar script played out before a fresh audience, one quick-thinking student scooped up a few drops of blood from the floor and inspected them under a microscope. What he saw were nucleated ovalocytes—the kind of red blood cells present in fish, reptiles, and amphibians, but not typically seen in humans. Under gentle interrogation, the homeless man divulged his scheme: swallowing chicken blood minutes before coming to the ER each year and then vomiting it up publicly so he could enter the hospital and have a safe home for the cold months. The testing he tolerated in the hospital was apparently a small price to pay for some warm meals and a comfortable bed.

Narrated to everyone around the country as an example of a student who used his wits to consider even the unthinkable, the story encouraged us to look under every tree, at every lab specimen, and on every floor for the diagnosis before being satisfied. Deplorably, considerably less emphasis was focused on the homeless man's plight and the desperate condition that prompted his sad and unusual survival tactic.

Psyched Up and Psyched Out

One last loose screw in the trio is worth mentioning: I was a freshman student and eager to hang out around the ER to "catch a little action." One of the upper-level psychiatry residents took pity on me and agreed to have the orderlies partially clear some space in a large supply closet, furnishing it with a small table and a few chairs. My job that Saturday night was to see patients in rotation with the two residents and to take a brief history from those coming to the ER with some psychiatric complaint. Once I had identified the patient's chief complaint, I was to call in the residents, who would fill in the details and determine a triage strategy. The whole scheme seemed rather jolly to me, as it allowed me to feel a little bit like a real doctor. So I nestled snugly in the closet like a mother bird waiting to hatch her eggs, surrounded by shelves bulging with supplies of fluid bottles, IV poles, ancient EKG machines, and dying ventilation equipment.

The very first patient ushered into my makeshift office was a large man and his petite wife, but by *large*, I mean more of a mountain of a man. His XXL sports coat refused to allow his arms to bend; his neck had disappeared years ago in the weight room. I concluded that this patient must have been a former NFL lineman, well dressed, and serene... at first. Although his wife took a seat as I asked her to do, the man remained standing, edgy, almost brittle, visually dissecting me, my small desk, and my squeaky swivel chair. He had the look of an over-muscled, anabolic steroid addict.

"Tell me about your situation," I inquired, parroting the phrase I had been assured would guarantee an open dialogue. Eyebrows raised, I tried to look both intent and perceptive beyond my years.

What happened next is not easy to explain. If you remember the gruesome scene in *Raiders of the Lost Ark*, the first Indiana Jones movie, in which the Nazi's face melts upon opening the lost Ark of the Covenant, you may better visualize the contorted expression I now confronted.

"I see the body of Jesus there on the ground, and you killed him... and

I'm going to get you for it!" he growled, swelling like a puffer fish to further expand his nightmarish dimensions and dwarfing both his wife and me.

I flashed a frantic look toward the only exit, but his huge body already partially blocked the way, and he began pushing equipment in front of the door. Trying to grab hold of the reins of my runaway fear, I prayed that my skin-deep composure would not be unmasked. The man was sweating profusely, his neck veins bulging, nostrils flared, and eyes as wild as a cornered wolverine's. I sensed he was losing screws by the second and was about to become totally unhinged. Under usual circumstances, the psychiatric interrogation rooms were outfitted with a panic button, a buzzer to call in the troops during times like these. My pretend office, sad to say, so recently improvised for me, did not have one. I must admit my future looked bleak. I fully believed that if I did not come up with something soon, things would not go well. Risking everything, I ran with the following.

"Hold on there just a minute. Are you Mr. Jones?" I asked quizzically, eyes widened, brows raised, and head slightly cocked in a sudden air of discovery.

The diversion derailed him for a brief second.

"No," he snorted, impatient and exasperated, "I'm Mr. Smith, you idiot!"

"Ah," I responded nonchalantly, finger pointed in the air, "then I must have the wrong room!"

And with that microsecond head fake, I brushed past him and slipped out the door to safety. I then dispatched four orderlies to the room to sedate the hulk before he injured his wife or some other naive medical student. He was admitted with a diagnosis of acute paranoia, and I ended my brief fascination with the world of the insane.

ER: Cases from the Knife and Gun Club

That was my first real-life lesson in trying to stay balanced while the sea was roiling violently in the storm. The experience proved valuable during my internship when I was twice threatened with a gun at close range in the emergency room, once for refusing to prescribe amphetamines for an addict, and another time for sewing up extensive lacerations on a young woman's face caused by her boyfriend who thought she had been unfaithful to him.

Most observers will agree there are loose screws all over the country, but there is no place like the emergency room to amass an entire hardware-store collection. I attended to some patients who set out on a journey to escape, and others with a death wish who swallowed battery acid; injected intravenous milk, turpentine, or mayonnaise; or smoked frozen cigarette papers packed with a mixture of marijuana and crushed aspirin tablets soaked in formaldehyde.

A colleague recounted a time when police informants warned that members of the La Raza Nation gang were conspiring to rush into the ambulance entry and roll a grenade into the ER. The staff practiced a disaster plan during which someone tossed a ball into the ambulance bay, and this intern's assignment was to kick it back outside. He wasn't sure, but it did seem to him as though the intern was considered the most dispensable member of the team. Fortunately, the plan was never put to the test.

Late one night on my watch, a man in shock was brought in by the police. He had been shot twice—once through a lung and once through a kidney. I inserted two chest tubes, began a transfusion through a central IV line to stabilize him, and then wheeled his gurney into the elevator to transport him emergently to the operating room. The elevator stopped one floor short of my destination, and the doors opened to reveal the patient's assailant. Enraged and with blood-red sclera, the gunman swept me aside with one arm and pumped one more, fatal bullet into his prey before racing off. My eyes were shut tight during the whole grisly incident, anxious to separate myself from the crime as a self-preservation technique. To my knowledge, the felon was never apprehended, there was no police lineup, and I was never interrogated. Loose screws everywhere!

CHAPTER 11

HISTORY TAKING:
A HEARING TEST FOR THE DOCTOR

No sooner had we arrived at school when the curriculum called for us to visit the wards, with the intention of practicing communicating with patients in the most rudimentary way. Having a simple talk with someone suddenly felt eerily foreign. No physical exams, no precise history, just conversation and dipping a first toe in the water. With a ratio of four freshmen to one clinician, we were escorted into the hospital to start asking questions. My instructor happened to be (you guessed it) a practicing psychiatrist. We were led, like children on their first field trip, into the locked psych ward, an environment quite different from the wards of today. As we crept skittishly down the hall, I noticed several sets of eyes peering at us through the slots in the doors that housed the unknown. Our teacher was on the prowl to cull prospective patients for us to interrogate.

We were approached almost immediately by an aggressive elderly woman propping her bifocals atop her head, a whistle dangling from a yellow lanyard, and carrying an official-looking clipboard. I took her to be a senior social worker or head nurse.

"Where's the fire?" she blurted out, her head beginning to rotate like a police strobe light.

"Right this way," urged the clinician with a knowing smile. Gently holding her at the elbow, he ushered her to her room and beckoned one of us to close the door.

The psychiatrist then turned to me to begin probing the very first patient I would ever question. Not surprisingly, my mind went blank; I had not the faintest idea what to ask, flustered by the patient's frantic demeanor and, to be honest, the aura of the ward itself. I needed a minute (perhaps even a few months) to collect myself.

"What brings you to the hospital?" I finally stammered (she spared me the often-quipped answer of "a taxi"). After that opening, I went numb and could not absorb a single answer that followed.

The next twenty minutes were a blur. This seventy-eight-year-old manic grandmother rattled off a breathless barrage covering, among other things, her purported sexual exploits with an entire Harley Davidson motorcycle gang, her publication of dirty literature that she sent to boost the morale of our troops in Vietnam, and the explicit foldout photographs of her posing for *Hustler* magazine. She interrupted the manic explosion only three times to ask briefly, "Do you understand?"

Like the proverbial bobble-head dog on the car dashboard and with my mouth half open, I nodded uh-huh.

She motored on, pedal to the floor, disgorging a flight of ideas. After leading me by the nose down the road to confusion, if not perdition, she paused, smiling coyly.

"You didn't understand a word I said."

Game over. She was right. With the implicit permission of the teacher, Grandma had taken me on an exhilarating ride and demonstrated to my three smug classmates how not to interrogate a patient. Mortified for having frozen so obviously in the line of rhetorical fire, I was mercifully given a reprieve. The psychiatrist explained to us that the vital counterpart to asking a good question was listening for an honest answer. And if the answer was nonsensical, we had the license to interrupt, clarify, or simply interject with something like, "That sounds crazy to me."

That day I learned not to add my own assortment of screws to the rest of the communal stockpile. I also learned that a nonanswer to a pointed question only translates into a worthless nonhistory. I pledged to never again be content with deflection or permit misinformation or misunderstanding to go unchallenged. This would prove invaluable when we students would next be charged with mastering the art of taking a precise and comprehensive patient history, from head to toe.

BOTH THE FOREST AND THE TREES

It didn't take long to be assigned my first complete history and physical of a flesh-and-blood patient. In just the second week of school, a first-year resident invited me to elicit the history of a woman in her mid-forties who was hospitalized with chronic active hepatitis. I knew by the sound of it that this illness must be something bad—and "bad" just about summarized the entire scope of my knowledge. Fidgeting with the loose button on my short white lab coat, I exchanged a few pleasantries with her while trying my best to appear professional. Fat chance. On my own, and face-to-face with a stranger whose body and life I was directed to get to know deeply, my brain was pounding. During college, I had relied heavily on my good memory to get me through my classes. But now I could recall only the opening line of my interrogation: *Tell me about your situation.* After that I went blank. The words, the sequence, the logic, the verbal algorithm slated to march me toward a diagnosis only swirled in my head; I could close my eyes and imagine myself inspecting a row of laundromat dryers spinning their loads of clothes.

Pretending to be paged, I awkwardly excused myself from the bedside at least three times to rush to the resident at the nurse's station to ask about the usual signs and symptoms of hepatitis, the hallmarks of the diagnosis, so I could interrogate the patient more effectively. After an hour of coming and going and painstaking data collection, I was ready to present my findings to the resident. Proudly summarizing all the classical features of hepatitis, I was caught off guard when he asked if I had noticed any other peculiar, prominent symptom in particular. Again I drew a blank.

The woman, the resident noted pointedly, had the mental age of a six-year-old. This observation would have been obvious to any untrained passerby from a brief conversation with her, but focusing as I had on hepatitis alone blinded me to the rest of her story. She was certainly answering all my questions, but it was the *way* she answered them that I had missed. I had not yet learned to improvise, to expect the unexpected. *To listen.*

A Day at the Improv

THOSE VERY FIRST PATIENT HISTORIES are usually seared into the memories of doctors who have gone on to take and forget hundreds more. And most of those practitioners will recall both the intimidating and awkward moments as well as the thrilling and awesome realization that someone was entrusting himself into their care—or as a young partner of mine remembers telling himself back then, *I can't believe this person thinks I will be able to help them.*

Often, coming up with workarounds can be as necessary as going by the book. As my young partner recalls, you can try to force information into a classical history and physical, but patients don't always fit the perfect script; their thoughts and stories must be directed.

A colleague reflecting on his own first patient experience recalls how his resident thought it might be amusing to assign him a patient and his wife who were both deaf and could only sign in Spanish. Determined not to show weakness, he spent most of the day inventing his own sign language: pointing to parts of their bodies that they would both nod either yes or no to. It worked well enough and underscored for him the need to be prepared to improvise.

Having to ask intimate questions of a stranger or even a casual acquaintance is yet another source of discomfort that new students must learn to overcome, along with developing an ear for the veracity of any forthcoming information.

Eclipsing the experience of the journalist who interrogates someone for a newspaper article, the doctor probes into a patient's health and relies

HISTORY TAKING: A HEARING TEST FOR THE DOCTOR

on getting answers that are truthful. The questions she poses are often more private, more embarrassing than those asked by a different kind of interviewer. The doctor-to-be must learn not to accept a deflection or a nonanswer, as well as to fully understand the degree to which the highly personal nature of the interview is usually punctuated by the disrobing of the patient. Processing the answers to closely held, confidential questions, the first-year student must balance sensitivity and tact with directed objectivity. To that end, freshman students are still guided, as I was, by Brian Bird's small, pithy monograph *Talking with Patients* on how to deal with the sometimes-delicate aspects of an interview.

I read the book before I ever met the first person I would question, and some of the chapters were, frankly, terrifying. Topics include how to handle any number of potentially discomfiting cases—the amorous patient who misinterprets the intimate questions and imagines the physical exam as an erotic opportunity; the dependent patient who confuses love with gratitude for his doctor who "saved my life"; the violent or belligerent patient who believes her condition has been worsened by her doctor or who wages war against her sad diagnosis; the litigious patient who conspires to entrap his doctor; the passive-aggressive patient who seeks to manipulate his doctor; the sociopath, the addict, and the patient who abandons advice out of fear.

I have experienced pretty much all of the above prototypes—except for that of the amorous patient, for which I am not sure I should receive congratulations or condolences, but for which I am grateful. The others have always required calm whenever calm is possible, as evidenced in a colleague's recollection of his early experience with a belligerent patient.

"My first contact with a psychiatric patient was with a paranoid schizophrenic; I was forewarned that these are the ones to avoid. We were two students and a psychiatry resident in a closed room. When the resident left the room for a moment, leaving us alone, the patient suddenly tried to punch me in the jaw, but I leaned back and he hit the other student, knocking him to the floor. I tried to block out what happened after that.

Another violent psychiatric patient stabbed a moonlighting student in the VA hospital ER while I was doing an EKG."

The theoretical goal of straightforward managing accompanied by clearly articulated thoughts and plans is not always achievable during these moments of terror or confusion, yet leaving vague, ambiguous messages to a patient's flawed assumptions is potentially dangerous. Be precise, I was taught.

Sure, but when I first asked Hurly Mountain—a writhing, alcoholic ex-middle-weight wrestler who had been dumped in a snowbank—where his pain was localized, he cried, "All over!"

I pleaded, "Could you be more specific?"

He insisted, "Top to bottom, inside and out."

"I hate to pin you down like this, pal, but does any place hurt more than any other?"

"Okay," he demurred. "Front to back and side to side."

In this case, Hurly's unhelpful generalizations fortunately proved to be non-life-threatening; like many patients we attended, Hurly was just pitifully negotiating for a warm bed away from the snow and the perils of the night.

THE COST AT ANY PRICE

WHEN I FIRST BEGAN TO PRACTICE MEDICINE, I took care of an eighty-five-year-old retired general practitioner, affectionately known as Buzzy. Universally loved in the community, he had a famous bedside manner and a marvelously dry wit. His timing was impeccable. I bumped into him at the opera one evening, where we shared a cup of coffee at intermission, and I took the opportunity to ask him about some of his most memorable doctor-patient relationship stories. Here is the one that showcased his ability to negotiate a potentially awkward interchange: Over a fifteen-year period, Buzzy had taken care of a man who always came to the office in an argumentative mood. He may have even been one of the original inventors of the conspiracy theory of medicine. It seemed that every time he was seen, the patient never failed to ask, "How much is this going to cost me?"

There was never an office visit, a blood test, an x-ray ordered, or a medication prescribed without his badgering, "How much is this going to cost me?" Displaying unflagging patience in the face of this predictable verbal assault, the doctor always managed a smile and calmly (or politely) offered the patient the information he demanded.

Quite by chance, one evening the doctor and his patient found themselves sitting at adjacent tables at a charity fundraiser attended by several hundred people. The yet-to-be served dinner menu was typical: mixed green salad, filet mignon, roasted potatoes, asparagus, flourless chocolate cake, and wine... lots of wine. The silent auction delayed the start of the main program, and the wine continued to flow.

While the dinner was finally served, the lights were dimmed for viewing an informational video. The audience was riveted by the images highlighting the desperate needs of the charity, but Buzzy's attention was trained on a faint strident noise with which he had become familiar. Looking over to the next table, he saw his patient slumped over his plate. Rushing over to the chair and gathering information quickly, he realized the man was suffering from what is often referred to as a "café coronary"—a large wad of steak had lodged in the man's throat, obstructing his breathing. The man's face had already begun to turn an ash-blue slate that was visible even in the darkened room; his respirations had all but stopped, and he was now comatose.

The doctor had been around a few steak dinners during his years of practice, so he had extensive experience when the situation called for the Heimlich maneuver. Just a few powerful tugs on the upper abdomen, and the offending bolus of meat catapulted out of the patient's mouth and onto the table. Sitting on the ground now with his patient's head and torso cradled in his arms, the doctor vigilantly monitored the resumption of breathing and the recovery of consciousness. As his eyes focused and his mind began to reconstruct what had just transpired, the patient's first slurred, raspy words were, naturally, "Doctor, how much is this going to cost me?"

Grinning as though he had been anticipating this question for the past fifteen minutes but having waited for this opportunity for fifteen years, the doctor replied, "About half as much as you would have been willing to pay me ten minutes ago."

The Whole Truth and Nothing But

WHILE NOT SPECIFICALLY TRAINED as history takers, jury panelists intuitively understand how the transmission of both verbal and nonverbal communication provides a deeper insight into the truth. Observing the uncomfortable posture, the furtive look, the nervous smile, the sweaty brow of a witness, jurors sift through the details of a testimony and absorb the cues that are either believable or not. Of course the panel has the advantage of conferring among themselves, sharing perceptions, ruminating on the display of evidence, and confirming each other's instincts. Moreover, they have the luxury of time to weigh both fact and hunch before arriving at a verdict.

The medical student honing the skill of taking a history also imbibes more than just words. She soon learns to read the facial expressions of her patient, feels the static in the air, intuits the squirm of family members in the room as she scratches below the dermis with sensitive mental fingers. She may ask the patient a question, receiving one answer but perceiving an opposite response from a loved one in the adjacent chair.

As a cardiologist, I have often asked about a patient's smoking history, diet, alcohol use, drug abuse, anxiety level, compliance in taking medication, or exercise habits. Turning to the spouse to confirm the answer, I might catch a furtive glance, a frown, an eyeroll that would help me arrive at a different conclusion. During hospital rounds, students are baffled, even aghast by how often their attending physician asks a patient the identical question they just posed an hour earlier but elicits a totally different response. Here is a common example:

HISTORY TAKING: A HEARING TEST FOR THE DOCTOR

"Have you ever had a history of seizures?" asks the student.
"Nope," replies the patient.
"Well, how about epilepsy?" persists the student.
"No, I never have," confirms the patient.
"Tremors?"
"No, sir."
"Fits?"
"None!"
"How about convulsions? Have you ever had convulsions?" presses the attending physician.
"Oh, *convulsions?* Sure, I've had *convulsions* ever since I was a kid and got knocked unconscious during a football game."

Similarly, in extracting symptoms of possible coronary artery disease, I might ask if patients have had any of the following: chest pain, pressure, tightness, or heaviness. Some would deny all the above but admit to a "squeezing-like" feeling. Sometimes only the patient's wife will nod a silent assent. On other occasions, the patient might adamantly disclaim any of the above... unless I specify if the symptoms have occurred during exercise.

"During exercise? Oh sure, I get all of those with exercise!"

Taking a comprehensive history requires the use of synonyms, hoping to purchase a patient's real understanding of what is being asked, and then clarifying what is received. The disavowal of a past history of hypertension may revert to an admission of a history of high blood pressure. Patients do not always lie when they tell us an untruth; something may have just been lost in translation. I discovered the literal reality of this phenomenon in the first few weeks of school.

I was given permission to travel to the deserts of Chihuahua, Mexico, once a month with a group of thirty-five nurses and physicians who called themselves the Flying Samaritans. They erected a few very rudimentary temporary clinics in this desolate area to provide healthcare to an indigent population. My job was not therapeutic, since I had only just finished college and knew nothing about caring for the sick. I was, however, fluent in Spanish, so translation was my primary contribution to this humanitarian effort.

Despite the inhospitable terrain of a sparsely populated wasteland, people seeking us out seemed to materialize from behind saguaro cacti and other parched scrub brush. The lines began forming before sunrise, and among the earliest patients I saw was a leathered middle-aged woman, facial wrinkles as deep as arroyos, who was accompanied by her preteen daughter. While rock climbing with her friends, the girl had fallen and sustained a hairline fracture of her right wrist. I was beyond thrilled when one of the residents showed me how to set the bone and apply a chic French-blue-colored cast. The girl was all smiles, delighted with the plaster trophy that she flaunted to her friends, and I had a sneak preview of the immense gratification one feels by having actually cured someone.

The girl's mother, however, was there for an entirely unrelated reason. It seems that her daughter was only one representative of the rest of the family—thirteen children in all, and still counting. The woman had neither the knowledge about contraception nor the ability to procure any of the alternatives. And as for her husband, "Not tonight, dear" was an unacceptable option. Consequently, she had conceived on an almost annual basis and was petrified that there were still more ova left to fertilize. She was now imploring me to help her shut down the factory without denying her husband access to the night shift.

In my best Spanish, I explained that if she took these birth control pills on a daily regimen as I prescribed, I could promise her success in limiting her family to what was now a complete soccer team, plus two substitutes. A broad, exhausted, grateful smile blossomed across her face. She clutched the pills like a jewel thief, bowed reverentially, and disappeared from the tent.

Six months later, the woman returned to display her traitorous abdomen, pregnant once again despite all that tribal councils, potions, and even my American medical science had to offer—and she was furious with me. I escorted her gently to one side of the tent to ask why she had stopped taking her pills. Had she met resistance from her Catholic priest or objections from her husband? She swore to me that she had followed instructions implicitly. I had told her to take one pill each day, and she did just that: She inserted one pill every day... *vaginally*. I had not specified the route of administration, naively assuming she would know. She not unreasonably supposed the pill would be most effective at the site of highest sperm concentration. Somehow, in the absence of a common oral tradition, the notion of oral contraceptives had been lost in translation.

Divided at Times by a Common Language

Encountering medical problems that emanate from social issues became a contemporary focus of attention in our curriculum and in others across the country. The newly developed community medicine class had us students following visiting nurses on their rounds to underserved populations. I soon learned that instructing patients to take a specific medication with each meal sometimes translated into just once a day. These challenges have garnered much-needed attention in today's training programs.

Given the complexity and nuance of language, is it any wonder that innuendo, misplaced memory, or anxiety provokes misperception? Scientific terms can often be misunderstood, medication regimens can be challenging, and disease itself may play a significant role in hindering precise communication. Thus, when the distraught elderly rabbi with atrial fibrillation learns he must be converted by his cardiologist, he asks frantically, "What will I be then?" Using every modality at our disposal, verbal and nonverbal, we may still fall short of effectively transmitting vital information and instruction. In unintended and subtle fabrication, the dissemination of false facts and imagined history (as well as conflicting opinions offered by various medical consultants) takes on the flawed character of the old game of telephone. It may sound humorous in retrospect, but I have on more than one occasion been confronted by a distraught father asking me if it was still absolutely imperative that I perform a "cardiac castration" rather than a "catheterization" on his son.

Bridging the scientific language barrier between patient and doctor has always presented a communication predicament, but perhaps an even more common cause for confusion takes place when shocking diagnostic news temporarily uncouples a patient's ability to process fact. Much as a flash of light can blind or a loud noise deafen, patients may temporarily lose their receptive powers... including their recollection of crucial advice.

During my pediatrics rotation at Guy's Hospital in London, I learned that the senior staff used to schedule a series of four interviews with parents whose children had just been diagnosed with the inherited, life-threatening lung disease, cystic fibrosis. This because the initial horror of the news left parents so dazed that it impeded their ability to assimilate any of the data presented to them during the first three sessions. Taking the visual pulse of the parents during these sessions helped the doctors determine when families had correctly incorporated the necessary information. In today's world, however, history takers are at a bit of a disadvantage.

Many patients complain that the introduction of electronic medical records has insinuated itself into that intimate ceremony we call history taking. Some doctors walk into the exam room carrying a computer tablet, asking questions, and typing answers into the electronic record but rarely look up. Receiving most of the attention, the computer has replaced the patient.

Not only is the personal touch diminished, but the subtle clues that might provide real insight into a patient's true responses are blunted. As mentioned earlier, the nonverbal communication between doctor and patient or patient and family, the looks of confusion, fear, anxiety, or misunderstanding, go unnoticed. The eyes that could melt a spouse's panic, the smile that could transmit calm, the wink that could broadcast confidence, the glance that could channel compassion—all these may still be present. But many patients relate that the fluidity of the emotional contact they crave and rely upon has now taken on a staccato tempo. The frenzy of entering data, filling in boxes to satisfy an electronic taskmaster, and justifying a billing platform becomes an intrusion on the candid, sensitive, and revealing nature of an office visit. Welcome to the downside of technology.

Because there is such an unfiltered imbroglio of medical information available to patients, physicians should feel the need to decipher the question mark on a patient's face now more than ever before. Despite having repeated this mantra over and over again to myself during my student years, I have since experienced occasions even recently when enough was apparently still not enough. I never used a computer tablet while taking a history or even during an office visit. Having to recall details of an interview that I dictated immediately afterward was one way to force myself to listen closely to the story. And I hoped that my face-to-face interaction would allow me to always identify and thwart misconception. But today's patients are pelted with medical advice, and sometimes the conspiracy theory can worm its way into a patient's cerebral nucleus of poor judgement.

Here's an example: A seventy-year-old woman presented to my office with multiple cardiac risk factors including reproducible blood pressures of nearly 300/140 mmHg. I hospitalized her to acutely control her staggering hypertension and prescribed a range of medications that she tolerated well. Two months after discharge, she was rushed to the emergency room with massive hypertension and a ruptured plaque in her right iliac artery that had blocked blood flow to her entire leg; the obstruction had taken place for a period long enough to devitalize her leg. She now required an amputation at the midthigh level. With one hand grasping the guardrail, I walked briskly along, maneuvering her gurney toward the OR, wondering where things had gone awry.

"The vascular surgeon tells me you stopped taking your blood pressure meds last month. Why in the world would you do that? Didn't we have a serious conversation about your risks?" I demanded, probably showing more frustration and less compassion than was appropriate.

"Well, when I went to fill the prescriptions, I got all this information and all the warnings about side effects from the Walgreen's pharmacist," she screamed, shaking uncontrollably and shoving a large fistful of half-crumpled papers in my face. "I was scared to death!" she continued. "If you had read this stuff, you wouldn't take these medicines either!" she screeched, now being wheeled into the pre-op area. "What did you expect me to do?"

"Call me!" I then added with all the calm I could summon. "I expected you to call me. In their zeal to inform their clients about all the details of the drugs they sell you, pharmacists sometimes fail to realize that a good physician has already weighed the risk-reward ratio before prescribing these meds. I am sure they believe they are providing you with a comprehensive service by describing all the potential side effects, and sometimes that warning is vital. What they do not tell you is what the danger is of *not* taking the medicine. And sadly, you have just learned that lesson."

I had failed to grasp the more covert signs, failed to foresee the possible misgivings, the foreboding that my patient must have intimated about the drugs. And by not digging deeper, I did not anticipate her abandoning a regimen that might have saved her leg. Too much information, especially when not properly interpreted, can be perilous, and the fear it generates can become a powerful, toxic repellent.

Clearly, no system is flawless. "Techno-nihilists" will decry the interposition of the machine in obstructing doctor-patient connectivity; tech-driven practitioners will point out the value of advanced informatics. The computer tablet can be used to remind the doctor of a patient's allergy history, alert him to an adverse drug-to-drug reaction (sometimes a culprit concealed in polypharmacy), and more easily track trends in hypertension, cholesterol management, anemia, or diabetes control. Computers spit out prescriptions that are legible, track outcomes, and obviate the need to decipher the poor penmanship of a colleague's notes.

I am reluctant to cheerlead one approach over the other, but instead would advocate for both technology and time-worn communication methods to blend the accuracy and the intimacy of the doctor-patient office experience. Taking a history "the old-fashioned way" by listening, not typing, gives both parties the satisfaction felt when two humans meet someplace in the middle... and communicate. Turning subsequently to the electronic medical record to document, track, and devise a plan of action adds structure to an otherwise potentially chaotic chart.

Despite using the most personal techniques of communication, chaos can still slither its way into the therapeutic agenda when history *taking* does not also involve history *listening*. Numerous examples come to mind, a testimony to the pressures placed on the physician to "hear between the lines." Sometimes taking a history is more than merely writing down words; it is perceiving thoughts and feelings that may not be adequately expressed verbally. A patient's ideas, worries, confusion, or cries for help may be begging us to be decoded.

A woman of only marginal allure married a truly handsome fellow and lived in profound and irrational fear that she might lose him to another woman someday. Her appearance deteriorated even further after having two children, and her panic became progressively desperate. It was at that point that she put herself to bed with complaints of paralysis of both legs. This psychogenic illness lasted for ten years, stoked by her premonition that, if she were to recover, her husband would leave her once he felt no further moral obligation to care for her.

Every attending neurologist and psychiatrist who saw her failed the moment they challenged her diagnosis rationally. The introductory line, "There is really nothing physically wrong with you" posed an impediment that the patient made insurmountable. Their very first contract was broken before it began, and the fortress of psychic disability became further entrenched. Then one day one of my psychiatry professors (an expert in crisis intervention) was consulted, and after truly listening to her history, he adopted a different tactic.

"I can see from your medical record that you are virtually paralyzed," he said, signaling for the first time a covenant of collaboration, an alliance, an apparent understanding of the patient's plight.

"The situation must be very difficult for you," he added. "What are the kinds of things that you wish you could do but that your condition prevents you from doing?"

"Well," she thought aloud, "I wish I could cook our meals, clean the house, look after the kids, and carpool."

"Gee, if that's all I had to look forward to, if I were you, I'd rather stay in bed!" observed the doctor. "Now tell me what you *really* wish you could do."

"Okay," she said, blushing and smiling demurely. "I wish I could go out for dinner, go to a movie, go dancing …" her voice trailed off.

Perusing the list and choosing the simplest, most positively reinforcing activity, the professor said, "You must, of course, stay in bed until this weekend, but on Saturday, you must go out to dinner with your husband, but then come right back to rest. Do this several times before moving to the next item on the agenda you outlined. In the meantime, I will inform your family that I absolutely prohibit you from cooking, cleaning, washing dishes, or taking care of the children for the next six months. Doctor's orders! Is that clear?"

The next Saturday night, the woman and her husband followed directions, and within a few weeks the patient was recovering. The success of this case depended on the doctor becoming part of her solution, not just another member of an adversarial team.

CHAPTER 12

LET'S GET PHYSICAL

SOMETIMES THE BODY WILL RELINQUISH its subtlest secrets only under the methodical scrutiny of a thorough physical examination. For the fledgling medical student, her discovery of a physical finding that confirms a diagnosis confers an air of power. Mastering the skill to expose disease using only the senses becomes a potent motivator. Every student lives for the day when she might elicit a telltale physical finding that has been overlooked by her teacher and that changes the course of therapy.

    This careful ritual that doctor and patient perform serves more than one purpose. Of course, the most basic premise is that an expert examination may alert the physician to the presence of an underlying illness or condition even before symptoms or laboratory tests recognize the existence of a problem. A sentinel lymph node, a carotid bruit (vascular murmur), a small melanoma, a palpated abdominal aneurysm, a borderline enlargement of the spleen, small hemorrhages of the retina—each may provide a dire warning in advance of symptoms. Directing attention to such a covert process offers the potential to explore a disorder more specifically, more promptly, and more economically. The obverse is also true: An apparent abnormality noted incidentally on a routine laboratory test can be refuted or substantiated by a qualified physical examination, avoiding unnecessary interventions. Many an invasive pitfall was circumvented by a wise practitioner who distinguished a benign murmur from a serious one, an artifact from a real tumor. In contrast, a cursory evaluation or inadequate examination skills surrenders these advantages.

BEST INTERESTS AT HEART

AS A STUDENT, I WAS DRAWN to the field of cardiology because of the power of the bedside exam. Experts who commanded the exquisite sensitivity of feeling (palpation) and listening to the heart (auscultation) could literally place their hands on a patient's chest and predict the catheterization findings of complex congenital or acquired heart disease. Especially in the days when echocardiography was still quite rudimentary, teaching physical examination skills became even more vital. Students honed their cardiac exam prowess with punctilious focus, especially because they anticipated a time when they might find themselves in the hot seat by a professor demanding a diagnosis at the bedside. I have a personal example:

One of the senior cardiology fellows and I performed cardiac surgery on rat hearts during my freshman year as part of my research curriculum. Since he also made rounds on the clinical wards, the fellow often described some of the interesting patients he saw, after which I would race home to my textbooks to expand on what he had just told me. I also attended the Monday noon cardiology conferences at which a patient "unknown" to the audience and typically with unusual findings would be paraded before 150 physicians. The core of this conference was centered on the physical examination. While everyone plugged their stethoscopes into a central system so all could "listen in," a nervous cardiology fellow selected randomly from the audience would lead the room through an examination of the patient and arrive at a diagnosis. His conclusion was then compared with the correct one documented by the catheterization. Finally, the department chief (Dr. Eugene Braunwald) would lead a scholarly, extemporaneous discussion on this subject for the next hour.

One Friday afternoon, my surgical partner mentioned that he had seen a patient that morning with dextrocardia—a rare congenital condition in which the heart is flipped to the right side of the chest rather than positioned on the left. As usual, I visited this diagnosis in my textbook in greater detail later that evening. When the mystery patient was ushered into the conference room the very next Monday, I recognized him to be the same man described to me with this unusual condition. Those in charge of the conference slyly reversed the chest x-ray on the viewing screen to avoid giving away the diagnosis, and in part to trap an unsuspecting cardiology fellow. But in this case, no cardiology fellow was put on the griddle; in fact, neither was anyone at the resident, intern, or senior medical student level. Dr. Braunwald called on *me* to come forward to direct the examination.

A buzz rippled through the room. No freshman student had ever been put in this position, and the attendees were anticipating an uncomfortable if not brutal public skewering. Much like asking a student to describe the retinal findings in a patient with a glass eye, dextrocardia was the other classic case used to impale a student whose exam skills were still green and easily tricked. But having recognized the patient's identity in advance, I appreciated that I was being handed an unexpected gift on a silver platter.

Working slowly, almost robotically, I began by pointing out that I could not palpate the heart in the usual left side of the chest, and that the heart sounds were louder on the right as well. As I built toward a climax, half the answer now clearly in sight, I asked the patient if he would mind dropping his drawers in front of this large group of physicians. Willingly, he complied. I revealed to the audience that the patient's right testicle hung lower than his left, concluding therefore that not only did he have dextrocardia, but that he also had situs inversus (a total mirror image of all his abdominal organs—liver on the left side and spleen on the right). For this I received a standing ovation from all except the chief, who merely nodded, his thumb characteristically stuffed into the inverted bowl of his empty pipe.

Most historians would agree that the golden age of bedside cardiology peaked in the 1950s in London with the emergence of Dr. Aubrey Leatham. Inventor of a must-have stethoscope and the first in the UK to implant a pacemaker, his skill in eliciting the most subtle physical findings was applauded worldwide, and this art was paralleled by his quick wit. He came to UCSD as a visiting professor when I was a second-year student, and during his brief visit he led ward rounds every day. Looking like the leading edge of a comet with a cluster of fellows, residents, interns, and students trailing behind him, Leatham glided from bedside to bedside examining patients. The residents who selected the patients gave Leatham no inkling as to the diagnosis, yet he effortlessly palpated, listened, and predicted the cardiac condition with a precision that inspired awe.

I was following along at the tail end of the comet when we stopped at the bedside of a twenty-year-old woman. Leatham palpated, auscultated with his signature stethoscope, and then to the amazement of all, put his ear directly on the patient's chest. He correctly announced that she had a congenital narrowing of her mitral valve and even quantified its severity with amazing accuracy. As the group moved on, one of the cardiology fellows summoned the confidence to probe.

"Dr. Leatham. Excuse me, sir. Did you really feel that in this case direct auscultation was superior to listening to the heart with your stethoscope?"

All chatter ceased, and the entire comet leaned in.

"No," he admitted with a grin and a dry British accent, "but when you get to be my age, it feels rather good to get a little tit in your ear every once in a while!"

Life has changed on the wards since those days, and what we might have found amusing and permissible at the time does us little credit when heard with contemporary ears. And yet I imagine other, perhaps less demeaning examples still percolate up as vehicles to diffuse some of the daily pressures.

My exposure to the potency of the cardiac examination through Dr. Leatham and others proved immensely valuable in future cases whose survival hinged on the accuracy of palpating and listening. A few months after joining a pair of clinicians in my first private-practice setting years later, I was asked to cover the office while the senior partners were on vacation. A young woman in her mid-twenties who had been labeled for years with a diagnosis of a serious congenital heart defect arrived for her annual appointment. Her complex condition had been based on the findings of an echocardiogram. Sadly, despite her persistent shortness of breath, she had been told that she was inoperable and that giving birth to children would be life-threatening—a painful prognosis, considering her recent marriage to a handsome firefighter and their fervent hopes to start a family.

As I listened carefully to the symphony of sounds made by her heart, I suspected that the conclusions drawn by the echo were subtly incorrect. The precise timing of her delicate heart sounds, nearly overwhelmed by loud murmurs, suggested a related but clearly different diagnosis, one that led me to believe she could, in fact, survive surgery. The revised impression was confirmed by a subsequent catherization, and she ultimately underwent a successful operation to cure her complex heart anomaly—and one year later gave birth to her "miracle child." Annually for more than a decade, the woman sent me a photograph of her son, which I displayed on my refrigerator door, a tender reminder of the power of the physical examination.

Flying without Instruments

Reliance on technology to answer all questions can have its perils, as we occasionally experience when a GPS has gone awry or a computer is on the fritz. We are prone to lose our bearings, office businesses screech to a halt, and the telephone numbers we once memorized are lost in the cloud. We feel isolated, impotent, incompetent in the world. Had we never been taught to navigate or calculate on our own, our plight would be even more dire on these occasions. Forgotten (or never acquired) basic skills leave many bereft of options or solutions with which to cope.

Ten years ago, I was on a Lufthansa flight to Johannesburg when the flight attendant called over the intercom at 1:00 a.m. for a physician to respond to an emergency. I worked my way to the back of the plane to an area near the small kitchen. There I found a middle-aged, morbidly obese Iraqi woman lying on the floor complaining of chest pain and struggling to breathe. Assuming at first that she was suffering from esophageal reflux, I gave her a trial of Maalox to treat her discomfort, and she appeared to recover. Unaccompanied on the flight and unable to speak English, the woman could not provide me with any information regarding her past history or the medications she was taking, which posed a challenge to my ability to develop a differential diagnosis. Since she seemed to improve during the next few minutes, however, the crew and I returned to our seats. Thirty minutes later, a second intercom call heralded her escalating deterioration.

The only other physician on the entire flight, an anxious-looking ophthalmologist, offered to get out of his first-class bed to help. I reassured him as I walked by that if the patient poked herself in the eye, I would call for him immediately. The woman had now collapsed on the floor and was deeply unresponsive. The German-speaking flight attendant handed me what seemed like a toy stethoscope that was even more useless given the din of the nearby jet engines transmitting through the floor. Similarly, the woman's enormous arms made negotiating their circumference with a blood pressure cuff an impossibility, much less obtaining a realistic pressure. The flight attendant swept to my side, efficiently proffering a suitcase containing an assortment of fifty identical clear vials hung with strict Prussian rigidity... and all labeled in German, with no English or generic translation. With clipped precision, she prompted:

"Which of these would you like to inject, Dr. Klein?"

Simultaneously, the pilot updated our whereabouts from the cockpit via phone to the flight crew as we were about to fly over open water, leaving the eastern shores of Newfoundland in our jet wake. Any instruction to emergently land the plane awaited my immediate decision. It was my call, suggested the captain, but it needed to be definitive... and prompt. If ever there was a metaphor that fit the designation "flying without instruments," this was it.

Armed only with the meager information emanating from an obese woman with a regular pulse and in a coma, I began to scroll through a mental list of the common ailments that could produce such rapid and profound physical findings with no focal neurological signs. I asked the flight attendant to inquire over the intercom if any passenger had a glucometer, and fortunately, one was soon produced by a retired nurse from South Texas. The patient's blood sugar was around 20 mg/dL—a profoundly low result, clearly the source of her coma, and one exposing her to permanent brain damage if not corrected immediately. On my knees, I was able to insert a central line in her internal jugular vein, procure several vials of D50 glucose from the flight attendant, and infuse a large bolus of this concentrated sugar solution, after which she sat bolt upright within minutes.

Had we abrogated responsibility for lack of, say, a CT scan, and delayed a diagnosis by diverting the plane to land in Canada, the woman would have suffered permanent brain damage, or even death. By the morning, she was sitting in her seat, eating breakfast—stable and grateful. Though our distant relatives might have been squaring off across a border somewhere in the Middle East at that very moment, medicine, as in sports, knows no racial, sectarian, or religious boundaries. The only foe is disease, and sometimes the only weapons with which to wage battle are our senses.

The Chance to Heal: A Touching Moment

THERE ARE NUMEROUS REWARDS that accrue from performing a physical examination. In his compassionate 2011 "A Doctor's Touch" TED talk, Dr. Abraham Verghese, a Stanford Medical Center infectious-disease consultant and author of the best-selling novel *Cutting for Stone*, describes his emotional connection with a patient slowly dying of AIDS. For months, the daily hospital encounters always included a ceremony, a kind of dance during which the doctor unbuttoned the patient's shirt, percussed, and listened to the chest with his stethoscope. In those days when the prognosis was dismal and the therapeutic options for AIDS were meager, this humane but futile pageant was more than a routinized performance; its function had little to do with the hope of some restorative discovery. The patient fully understood the display. The "laying on of hands" took on a secondary meaning; it rehearsed a tender reinforcement of trust and affection that ran deeper and stronger than the hopeless outcome portended.

Emaciated and too weak to speak during the final hours of his life, the patient summoned Dr. Verghese and pointed pleadingly to his chest with a frail, bony finger beckoning to the doctor to unbutton his shirt for the last time. The doctor complied, blessing him with this final tactile gift—his farewell touch. Having fulfilled his promise to his patient to bring all that medical science had to offer to the bedside, Dr. Verghese placed his hands gently on the patient's back, percussed lightly, listened solemnly, and reassured him that he would be traveling with him on his final journey.

I cannot say for sure whether the Healing Touch heals. I know that medical centers offer programs encouraged by doctors and nurses and demanded by patients. I know that if petting one's dog can lower one's blood pressure, if massage therapy can ease anxiety, and if the laying on of hands can invest people with hope and healing, then the capacity of touch to imbue energy, instill confidence, and establish a bond generates a force that is difficult to replicate. Can we prove that lives are lengthened? Perhaps not. Do we surmise that lives are enriched? So patients tell us.

Most mammalian infants develop normally and thrive only when they can maintain some physical contact with their kind. And even as an adult, one's continued drive to bond within a group is a primal force imperative to the maintenance of healthy adaptive behavior. An eight-week-old puppy reared in isolation will unwittingly stick its nose in the flame of a candle and fail to keep its immediate environment clean, lacking both precautionary information and rudimentary socialization skills. The more basic need, however, the desire to connect with others, is blunted when touch is withheld. There seems to be a common thread among mammals that craves a hand on the shoulder, a comforting hug, a pat on the back, a warm embrace. Studies have shown that holding hands lowers the stress hormone cortisol. When a teacher gently touches a student's arm, the pupil is more likely to participate in class, and a doctor's confident touch results in his greater acceptance by his patients. In this milieu, vital information is imparted. The response to simple tactile stimulation sends a message to the large vagus nerve to de-stress, relax, and encourage more subdued, mellow hemodynamics. Further, the release of the neuropeptide oxytocin, often referred to as "the cuddle hormone," engenders trust and a sense of connection.

No doubt Dr. Verghese's practice of examining his patients nourishes the faith they place in him, his touch rewarding their brains with a powerfully positive neurohormonal surge akin to the cortex's reactions to sweet tastes and enticing aromas. As I etched it into my routine as a student, I harnessed the value of touch and brought it to the bedside. During the years I performed heart catheterizations, I appreciated how consistent this asset was. Approaching the patient who was already draped and prepped on the table, I often witnessed how anxiety raised their blood pressure. Simply a soft voice and laying my hand gently on their leg or abdomen usually resulted in an immediate improvement in pressure and heart rate.

Data at Our Fingertips, but Still Out of Touch

The more computers and monitors render the doctor's morning hospital rounds almost superfluous, the less patients can count on the beneficial impact of touch. The argument: The remote harvesting of information by artificial intelligence is at the very least valid, and probably even more efficient than that gleaned manually. All of this may be true, but clearly the patient and his family sense the isolation it brings with it.

On the rise is the use of telemedicine, often providing critical healthcare support from a distance to underserved, destitute regions of the world. Pandemics such as COVID-19 depend heavily on virtual connections for information and care, as well as a distancing mechanism to protect healthcare workers from exposure to contagion. Distance medicine can be absolutely vital when the alternative entails a witchdoctor, a bone and a feather, the eye of newt, or an amulet, but it remains a necessary technology even though it magnifies the deprivation of touch to those who, in their squalor, often feel untouchable. It seems the height of irony that the word *covid* means "to see together" in Latin, yet the interdiction to visit, to touch, the commandment to live apart, imposes an almost satanic suffocation of our sense of well-being, our security of place. We repel touch and invite depression.

The coronavirus pandemic has done much to accelerate the general acceptance of telemedicine. As a vehicle for an annual checkup, pediatric visits, dermatology exam, or follow-up from surgery, for example, telemedicine represents the new normal—less cumbersome, more efficient, less expensive, and at times less risky. By downsizing the office footprint, both for square footage and staff, the doctor can offset what has been lost in reimbursement over the years. Patients feel less exposed to infection, maintain greater privacy, avoid travel cost and time away from work or home. Technological growth in this field is only just reaching its stride. Wearables monitor vital signs and oxygen saturation, cameras capture precise skin pathology, and telemedicine stethoscopes, otoscopes, and ophthalmoscopes investigate some of the rudimentary physical findings useful in diagnosing common ailments. Even if the more sophisticated remote devices (catheterizations, surgery) take some time to be perfected or accepted, many screening office visits will be well served. While the computer interface will impose its own stress on the doctor-patient relationship, requiring a doctor's reinforced emphasis on "bedside manner," the pressures of an evolving pandemic will undoubtedly change the business of medicine even during the better times that lie ahead. But there will be a human cost, particularly for those living with dire needs.

In Western medical circles, the choice is rarely all or none. Robotic surgery has captured the imagination of a public hypnotized by the very innovative nature of the concept, accepting if not demanding its use enthusiastically. Rapidly gaining in popularity for procedures such as prostatectomy, robotic surgery promises to displace the doctor even farther from contact with patients. Results are clearly dependent on the operator's exceptional training and experience. We are easily confused by mixed observations and contradictory data describing the value of robotics when metrics such as infection rate, length of hospitalization, blood loss, or expense are used. The human cost in eroding the doctor-patient relationship, however, seems evident, although certainly mandatory in regions where, given the maldistribution of healthcare workers around the globe, access to these procedures would not otherwise be available. Unquestionably, most surgeons employing robotic approaches offer their patients all the same personal hand-holding and confidence-building their conventional counterparts do. Sadly, however, we may yet see a scenario in which no doctor need ever touch a patient ... cortisol, confidence, or comfort notwithstanding.

It will always be possible to cherry-pick situations in which the ultrasound or other machinery is in error. Truth be told, in recent studies that compare accuracy, technology usually bests human diagnostic acumen, although there is considerable controversy as to which criteria are used in the comparative analysis. Often, physicians sacrifice effort and efficiency for outcomes, appearing to lose the battle to technology if time alone is the metric of interest. What a triumph this would represent if the goal of medicine were to be fast rather than correct! In a recent Harvard study, 234 physicians made half as many errors as computer-based platforms in diagnosing complex illness in 47 patients. Yet other studies confirm the superiority of computer-based interpretation of scans for breast cancer and lung tumors.

One additional caveat: Clearly, all diagnosticians are not alike, differing in their level of training, intuition, bedside manner, and willingness to remain current. Assuming a general level of competency, however, one might expect more uniformity of opinion among technicians than with a wider spectrum of human examiners. So here again, the drum I'm beating is less for "either-or" and more for "and." Careful, thoughtful, precise histories and physical exams help direct clinicians to order studies that confirm or refute and provide specificity that limits expense. Aside from the obvious adage that two heads are better than one, the sensitive, compassionate addition of the human touch is a bonus that is impossible to quantify. There is, of course, a cost: time expended on teaching and learning, and time, some would argue, that is "squandered" on an exam in the office. Conversely, if those extra minutes obviate the urge to throw the proverbial spaghetti of tests at the wall to see what sticks, and instead knowledgeably targets a specific problem, then time, money, risk, and pain are all saved.

CHAPTER 13

"IF YOU CAN'T GET ALL YOUR WORK DONE IN TWENTY-FOUR HOURS, YOU JUST HAVE TO STAY UP LATE"

During a sociology experiment that studied groupthink conducted at a college in New York, students (subjects) were asked to fill out a routine questionnaire while smoke was artificially pumped into their small classroom through an air-conditioning vent. Pretending to be applicants at the same time was a small group of coconspirators who were instructed to ignore the smoke. Taking a quick look around and seeing the others' failure to respond, the subjects continued to fill out their forms despite the perceived danger signals of a fire. The lesson: Group psychology—some would say "mob psychology"—sets the tone for much of our deportment. No one will throw trash on the street in Singapore; no one will cut in line in Tokyo. These things are just not done.

Similarly, appreciating how one's colleagues carry out their hospital responsibilities dictates one's interpretation of the code of honor at each training institution. Inheriting a sick, medically unstable patient from a careless intern who is anxious to go home informs the next intern about the rules of the road. Conversely, meticulous patient care and the pride of compulsion are ingrained in house staff by their colleagues in their working environment.

My recollection of my own house staff experience is that explicit

instructions for our professional habits never required exposition, never needed justification; they were simply guided by unspoken peer pressure. A few examples:
1. House staff would not go to sleep without knowing the results of an important laboratory test.
2. An intern whose night shift was nearly over would never transfer the care of an unstable patient to the colleague replacing him.
3. An intern covering night call for one of her peers would work extra hard to ensure that her colleague's patients did not endure a preventable complication under her watch.

I had a little one-upmanship going with an intern whose call schedule alternated with mine. Asked to examine one of his patients one night by the ward nurse, I took special interest in his patient's symptoms and appended a medical article about the disease to the chart for him to peruse the next day. He did the same for one of my patients a few nights later, and these extravagances escalated over the next few weeks. Hoping to put a cap on this time-consuming exercise when I saw a patient of his with restless legs syndrome, I wrote a ten-page summary of the subject in the chart, with references dating back to the early 13th century. It was all in good fun, all in exceptional learning, and all in great care. In the interest of time and to preserve our sanity, the competition was declared a draw and gracefully put to bed.

Married, or Married to Medicine?

SOMETIMES, HOWEVER, the price of the investment is too dear. The demands of time by one's peers often supersede those of one's family, threatening alienation and even divorce. One of the medical students working opposite me on a medicine rotation seemed to be bathed in misfortune. The patients assigned to him were always the sickest and consequently were inevitably delayed for discharge. As the weeks wore on and his patient load grew, he was at one time following nineteen patients on respirators and helping to cover a thirty-bed liver ward. Not surprisingly, he rarely made it home. His wife threatened divorce until our senior resident invited her to join us on rounds one morning at 6:00 a.m. (clearly a HIPAA violation that would be impossible to offer today). Seeing what her husband was expected to do every day gave her a deeper appreciation for his dilemma. Disease was the common enemy, the temporary thief of their home life. His absence there was a call to duty, not a choice.

Married in the first months of my internship, my own experience was quite similar. The one week of vacation time allotted to me for that year was used for travel to and from our wedding ceremony and for our forty-eight-hour honeymoon. Since I spent an average of 120 hours a week in the hospital, our "together time" consisted mostly of my new wife bringing dinner to the cafeteria to catch a momentary glimpse of me hoarding red- and purple-topped tubes of blood samples in my lab coat, while inhaling my meal at a record pace lest my pager call me away for the night. (How my eating habits had changed since the time when I was a young boy!)

After several months, we chose one Sunday when I was not on call to drive to the mountains for the day. I wanted to check to be sure my patients were stable before leaving, so I began making "quick" rounds at 5:00 a.m. with a promise to meet her at 9:00 in the hospital lobby. But every time I set foot in the elevator, a nurse would notify me that a patient had spiked a temperature of 103 degrees or precipitously dropped a blood pressure. By 3:00 p.m. I had not quite finished, so my wife resignedly collected our blanket and untouched picnic and dragged herself home. I joined her there just after 4:00. Furious about and disappointed by the events of the day, we walked back to the hospital together and each physically kicked the outside wall a few times. Learning to direct our frustrations at the hospital rather than each other became a valuable asset that preserved what was to become a forty-nine-year marriage... and counting.

Y Not? Approaching Gender Equality in Medicine

Out of aversion to this reality, a growing cadre of trainees have moderated attention and commitment to patient care to protect their own family life. Striking a balance between personal time and delivery of healthcare in today's world is more challenging than ever before. The very structure of family relationships is evolving, and the pressure on family cohesion has increased still further as more women are entering the classroom. I was informed that the first woman OB-GYN resident in the history of Baylor College of Medicine was admitted only in 1975, one year before the first female cadets entered the freshman class at West Point. This was also a time when only doctors (predominantly men) were allowed in the delivery room (no dads or doulas), breastfeeding was unusual, and the few women graduating from medical school were compelled to organize their office practices like those of their male counterparts.

Aside from the economic incentives that make hospital employment attractive, the change within the demographic makeup of medical trainees plays a part in current scenarios. In 1968, 15 percent of admissions to my medical school class were women—only slightly more than the average nine percent entering schools throughout the country. It may be convenient to explain this disparity based on a presumed lesser percentage of women applying, but it's problematic nonetheless, and wholly unacceptable. Applauding the trend in 2020 toward gender equality in medicine, slightly more than 50 percent of school admissions are now women. A source that continues to disturb, however, is the relatively minimal increase in Black and Hispanic women (or men) represented in admissions during this time; the gender rebalancing coming almost entirely from a twelve-fold rise in Asian women applicants. And yet the stresses imposed on women in the workplace continue to be especially taxing in a career path that is fraught with long hours, night call, emotional assaults, and unpredictable emergencies. Let me give you just one example of what one female student in our class endured during her first two years.

Jan became pregnant in her freshman year and took just enough time off to complete labor and delivery. Since her husband taught university in Palo Alto, she was the sole caregiver of her baby and was forced to return to school carrying him in her backpack. As the infant became more aware of his surroundings, he was exposed to any number of gruesome physiology experiments: strain gauges sutured onto the surface of a dog's heart, surgical procedures performed on fluffy bunnies. When the child was two years old, he watched as his mother inserted a tube into the jugular vein and across the tricuspid valve of a rabbit. She injected the ear vein with streptococcus, and a few days later the animal developed an infected heart valve, as anticipated. The experiment involved euthanizing the rabbit to examine the valve microscopically.

In contrast to the horror most children would likely express after witnessing the gruesome death by air embolism of a bunny rabbit, this toddler's unperturbed response was, "Can I have the eye?"

Overhearing this reaction in our pathology lab, I feared for the future psychological health of both mother and child. I had to acknowledge that although several male students had become fathers during medical school, none faced the same pressures of parenting tolerated by Jan.

According to a recent study referenced in *The Atlantic*, 40 percent of women physicians are either working part time or have retired within six years of graduation. This compares to approximately 3.6 percent of male physicians. Certainly, their desire to initiate a family while juggling an average of eight and a half more hours per week of household duties than their male counterparts exerts pressure upon women to constrict their professional careers. Once again, clinic affiliation and shift work scheduling provide more flexibility to accomplish these goals. After a few years of fulltime motherhood absent patient contact, however, women find that many states demand relicensing with updated board examinations. Often these obstacles prove too large a hurdle, and early retirement becomes the norm.

In an aging America whose increasing medical demands seem to be unmet due to maldistribution if not an outright physician shortage, the growing representation of women in the clinical field demands both attention and support. Patients have voiced a wish to select a doctor based on gender; for many, the decision is less dependent on diagnostic acumen than on maximizing one's comfort zone.

The cost in time, funds, and intellectual resources needed to train one doctor is enormous, and the student's investment in tuition, emotion, and effort is likewise exorbitant. Medical board examiners correctly recognize that even a two-year hiatus from direct clinical contact imposes a potentially significant gap in knowledge and technique that must be addressed conscientiously if patient care is to be safeguarded. Certainly, however, complete recertification seems over and above what should be required for women to reenter the medical workforce after pausing to build a family. By taking a short refresher course in their specific field, perhaps followed by a brief period of mentoring, women physicians could revive the diagnostic and therapeutic skills that had previously become almost instinctual, and they thus might be encouraged to resume their practice.

These days physicians of both genders are trending toward a shift work mindset, with training supplemented by the more efficient acquisition of learning by computer. Granted, this allocation of time provides a healthier home environment for the trainee. But is something vital lost? Is there a cost?

SEE ONE, DO ONE, TEACH ONE: THE VALUE OF EXPERIENCE

EVERY MEDICAL STUDENT OR INTERN will recollect a time at the start of an emergency room shift when a half-dozen apparent catastrophes were happening all at once: a multicar accident with patients in shock from blood loss, a busload of severely dehydrated hikers returning from Aspen with diarrhea from giardiasis caused by a liver fluke found in mountain rivers, a group of punk rockers overdosed on Ecstasy, a pediatric influenza epidemic, a mass shooting. Deciding which patients warranted attention first was easy: One just had to catch a glance from the head nurse in the ER. With a single nod, one knowing look, that ER nurse could suss out and signal which situation was most critical. The feel for triaging serious illness is more than merely good intuition. Just as the Metropolitan Museum of Art's Thomas Hoving famously had the uncanny ability to instantly detect whether a painting was a forgery, so too the head ER nurse will quickly parse the acute from the chronic. How? Experience. And there is no substitute for it. Experience cannot be taught; it must be lived.

Being a part of a large, busy medical center meant being in a position to identify and care for almost every major illness—the building blocks of precious clinical experience. In the search for the ideal teaching hospital, prospective interns scrutinize the number and diversity of the patient population they would care for in hopes they will be exposed to every kind of disease and trauma at least once. Required, however, is adequate time and opportunity to do so. The rate-limiting issue is always time. An internship lasts only a year, and there are multitudes of diseases and complications to confront. Because the uncommon or rare disorders don't present to the hospital every day, many interns will never have the chance to care for a patient with hemophilia, an unusual tropical fever, a bizarre fungal meningitis, or a rare congenital abnormality. I was terrified that if during my internship I did not learn to diagnose and treat every one of the more esoteric syndromes, I would suffer both embarrassment and ineptitude when as a resident I would be looked to for all information and guidance by my team. But it was not all about the exotic or unusual, either; sometimes even the most common problems could present with confusing similarities, which no textbook could adequately cover. For example, I could read about a patient who arrives at the ER with acute shortness of breath, but there is no true substitute for time on the front line, examining someone whose breath sounds are nearly inaudible and whose chest x-ray can easily be interpreted as either florid pneumonia or congestive heart failure.

The consequences of failing to correctly discern which is which are dire. A medical journal or book chapter offers only written information and will take you only so far, just as a lecture or essay describing a shade of red will suffer from an inability to distinguish magenta from scarlet, until that color is actually seen. So too a narrative may struggle to describe the subtle differences between a wheeze and a squeak, a rattle and a rub, and offer limited opportunity to inform a therapeutic decision.

The physical examination performed on the spot donates to the pool of experience, and experience can sometimes be a cruel teacher. The time needed to unwrap these lessons expended in the ER is both precious and limited. But equally precious is the time spent with one's own family. Most trainees now find themselves virtually bisected: head in the hospital, heart in the home.

The drive to amass experience by having cared for the most diverse population of syndromes was paramount. On some occasions when I was on call, I would bring a dozen doughnuts down to the ER to curry favor with the admitting second-year resident. Scrutinizing the list of patients on the blackboard to be admitted, I could often persuade him to assign me the juiciest cases. One of my colleagues functioning with the same intentions recalled fighting with an intern from Duke over who would get to admit a particularly interesting patient. Forty years after he'd forgotten the outcome of this skirmish he could still recall his race against time and the edge of hunger to wring the most experience from whatever opportunities could be had, and by whatever means.

Competitive by nature, most medical students find themselves comparing their skills and their reputations with their colleagues. Again, the prevailing milieu in each program dictates the proportionate distribution of time dedicated to head or heart. The fear of starting one's career as the dreaded "bad doctor" gnaws at every student's psyche. Any derogatory word around the clinical wards and on rounds can be caustic, but self-examination may be a harsher critic yet. Hours spent with family spawn guilt at being away from one's ill patients, during which time, being at home is not the same as truly *being in the present* at home. Spousal duties will surely erode the time available to build a store of knowledge. Attempting to do two jobs well adds to both physical and mental fatigue ... and fatigue becomes the thief of experience. These competing challenges can be as daunting as working the typical thirty-sixth hour of the day every other or every third day.

Exhaustion associated with long, continuous hours of training has been accused of leading to errors of judgment. How to correctly compare these errors with those caused by lack of experience and exposure to "enough" medicine is impossible to determine. We cannot be our own controlled experiment. If, for example, I had never been given the time/opportunity to attend a patient with an unusual presenting symptom of a disease, would I even recognize it at some point in my future practice? Which poses the greater threat: mistakes made by fatigue, or those made by lack of knowledge? I can only propose a personal comment.

Unfortunately, during my years of training and beyond, I have not been spared committing vital errors in judgment. But I can say that any mistakes I made were due to either my lack of knowledge or experience or my misreading of the clinical clues; I cannot remember ever having made an error because of fatigue. Asked whether they would rather be cared for by an intern who has been awake for ten hours or thirty-six, most patients would surely opt for the former. But when choosing between a graduate of today's training vs. a seasoned veteran of a brutal medical-training program requiring a thirty-six-hour schedule every other night, most would vote for the latter.

The details of how past and current program restrictions differ provide some insight into why medical practices are changing. As many of my colleagues can attest, the emerging new normal is the product of design by committee. Attempting to improve conditions for house staff, educational boards have imposed a structure that introduces a mix of habits both good and bad. As you will see, today's physicians tend to dance to a somewhat different tune.

CHAPTER 14

SISYPHUS, HERCULES, OR JOB: WAS IT ALL TOO MUCH TO ASK?

"A Hard Day's Night," ... "Eight Days a Week," ... "In the Midnight Hour"—so many of the songs composed by the Beatles, and one by Wilson Pickett seemed to sing directly to me during my life as an intern. Or, as I remember the destroyed look on the faces of weary interns after pulling a hectic night shift, perhaps *Look What the Cat Dragged In* would be even more descriptive. These tunes mirrored the plight of medical students and house staff across the country who averaged 120 hours per week in the hospital. The most prestigious internships could exact a price of night call every other night, but most settled for every third. Whether out of compassion or to attract good students, some institutions even opted for call every fourth night. Worn as a badge of courage, the thirty-six-hour-on/twelve-hour-off schedule infected some with a future chronic malady we have come to know as "doctor's disease." Encouraged by professors who themselves grew up in this completely immersive training environment, students who sought to emulate their teachers, to know one-tenth of what the chief knew, to be singled out as one of the "good students," willingly submitted to this brutality. As mature physicians, many continue to absorb as many patients into their practice as they are offered, regardless of their ability to control quality of care or juggle a healthy personal life.

The Report Card

ENTER THE ACCREDITATION COUNCIL for Graduate Medical Education (ACGME) in 1981. After extensive study and in an honest effort to minimize errors made by house staff fatigue, recommendations were made to standardize training programs for residents: Between 1988 and 1989, the eighty-hour work week was introduced, call schedule was capped at a maximum frequency of every third night, contingencies were inserted to mitigate fatigue or illness of the medical student or house officer (intern or resident), and adequate supervision was mandated. These specifications were further refined in 2003 as a common set of standards, later to include requirements for didactic lectures, reporting and communication systems, and open discussions regarding respect, honesty, privacy, compassion, and discretion in patient care.

The recent vocal objections to the typical 120-hour work week by young Goldman Sachs associates has captured the attention of CEO David Solomon and the media. Defended by their superiors as the training imperative to service their clients' every whim, this practice superficially mirrors the friction that exists between the old guard and the new in medical systems. Of course, the aspiring physician and the junior business associate each encounter significant differences in working conditions, pay scale, and—most notably—the irreversible consequences of making a fatal mistake. My colleagues nod, understanding the protests and acknowledging the distinctions.

To stress the importance of maintaining the same degree of respectful interchange between house officers and faculty that one offers one's patients, the council implemented a tool for residents to critique their instructors' performance in the form of a graded feedback, or report card. For instructors, many medical schools rely on physicians in private practice to provide clinical mentoring, capitalizing on their experience and using their hospitalized patients to supplement an intern's exposure to additional cases, offering sophisticated, often genteel, approaches to patient care, as well as practical career advice. This kind of tutoring can add vital enrichment, since some full-time academicians whose focus has been primarily on research may have less recently honed clinical skills. But because time and expertise are occasionally limiting commodities in the private sector too, one obvious reason for implementing the feedback afforded by such a report card is to ensure quality control.

Clinical instructors chosen for the teaching staff consider their appointment an honor, a testament by their academic peers of their currency with the medical literature and their value as physician role models. As we might sadly expect, however, some abuse this privilege. Didactic lectures take time to prepare and compete with a physician's busy office and hospital responsibilities, so residents are often directed to do the "grunt work" for their instructors, sometimes performing a patient's only in-depth history and physical examination. They are also expected to act as a buffer for their attendings when urgencies arise in the hospital at night, taking night call but receiving little teaching in return. The report card gives the house staff a real voice in disclosing these offensive habits and even recommending the discharge of chronic offenders.

There is a potential dark side, however, to this process. In an era when children have been raised with grade inflation and participation medals, a few residents use the report card as a cudgel to demand undeserved accolades from their teachers. They can discredit an instructor and threaten his removal from the teaching staff if he refuses to give the resident a better grade.

"It is impossible to get rid of an incompetent trainee," bemoaned a colleague and much-admired clinical professor at Baylor College of Medicine. "Fear of reprisal from a dissatisfied house staff has allowed the pendulum to swing far off center."

As former chief of one of the cardiology residency teaching programs in Houston for more than eighteen years, I recall threats of this kind becoming more prevalent over that time. I particularly remember an intern who refused to wait in the hospital past 3:00 p.m. to see a patient being flown in by helicopter with a dissecting (tearing) aortic aneurysm. His demeanor and eagerness to learn was marginal at best. At the end of the month when I gave him a C grade, he sought me out to demand I change his grade to an A. I explained that a C grade represented the work of someone who showed up every day and displayed the minimum level of interest and knowledge; an A would be awarded for insightful behavior, exceptional acquisition of knowledge, and improved bedside diagnostic and therapeutic skills. Fortunately, his complaints to the chairman of the residency program about my unfair assessment of him and my poor teaching ability landed idly, as positive evaluations from the other residents offset his accusations.

Nearer the end of this eighteen-year experience, I was called into the chief's office because several residents had complained about the "harsh" treatment they had received from Howard, one of my partners and an excellent teacher in the program. True, his manner was somewhat staccato, but never abrasive. The interns were nonplussed because he put them on the spot too often, demanded too much, and required consistent, high-quality performance. But he expected no less of himself. In addition to his appointed teaching hours, Howard volunteered to attend Morning Report every day, lavished a great deal of extra time on rounds, and displayed superior knowledge and diagnostic skills.

When the chief repeatedly demanded that I fire this physician, I refused. I observed that he represented the best of us and said that if I was forced to let him go, I would discharge myself and four other instructors as well. In reaction, we ultimately did leave the teaching program and were sadly replaced by a group willing to capitulate to the pressure of the house staff and offer applause that was not always deserved.

As a student in a hospital in London, I witnessed a registrar (resident) admonish a ward nurse for failing to carry out an important order he had entered in the chart of an unstable patient. Rather than apologize or explain her error, the nurse self-inflated to her maximum height and announced a strike. In a symphony of support, thousands of British nurses joined her and walked out of hospitals throughout the city. Here too we have come to a time when the voice of the house staff is strong and loud enough to potentially terminate good teachers and even jeopardize the accreditation of an entire residency program. For comparison, imagine a high school student demanding to have his report card embellished by threatening to have the school board rescind the school's accreditation.

Playing by the Rules and Bending a Few

To be fair, the rationale for each rule had its roots in responding to real abuse in isolated institutions. Take, for example, the eighty-hour week. Many residents used to work their typically oppressive night schedule but added a night or two per week of moonlighting to the mix. With pay scales so menial, neither single interns nor married couples could survive without supplementing salaries by working in an outside, private hospital at night. (As an intern, I was paid an annual salary of $7,800.) For residents with a young family shouldering the additional burden of enormous debt from college and medical school, there was no other way to keep creditors from the door. The new standards count hours of moonlighting into the total eighty-hour work limit, and the additional reimbursement responds to the needs of a growing family, in part offsetting tuition debt that often exceeds $250,000. Moonlighting was officially prohibited during my residency, although faculty usually turned a blind eye to violators, since the private sector covertly eased the financial burden of the academic institution whose budget could afford to pay only subsistence salaries to house staff.

I did not moonlight until my years as a cardiology fellow, but when I did I covered a twenty-two-bed ICU in a busy private hospital one night, the CCU at my academic institution the second night, and was free the third. Sometimes insomnia can be a blessing.

Further, by limiting the number of patients followed by each resident to ten and stipulating a fourteen-hour period of freedom after a twenty-four-hour shift, the council sought to minimize burnout and depression among staff. (Often as the result of depression, substance abuse, mood disorders, stress, long hours, sleep deprivation, and financial debt, suicide among physicians is the highest of any profession, exceeding even that of the military.) Respectful discussions were encouraged, thereby helping to blunt the fear of retaliation if a student questioned the opinion of senior staff. Such a policy would have been welcome during my years as a student.

As a senior student, I was admitting patients to the hospital one Sunday evening (patients were being often admitted the night before planned surgery). One week earlier, a twenty-four-year-old Asian man had undergone a catheterization and was diagnosed with severe narrowing of his mitral valve. The plan was to replace the valve first thing Monday morning.

The patient did not speak a word of English, so my assessment was based purely on a written history and my examination. But when I motioned for him to disrobe, he removed his shirt in two milliseconds, his movements lightning quick, his reflexes twitching to attention, and his sinewy muscles rippling with hyperactivity. As I suspected, the patient was in thyroid storm—a metabolic condition that dramatically increased cardiac output and blood flow across the valve, registering a more severe degree of valve obstruction than was the case and fooling his cardiologist into believing his valve required replacement.

I cancelled the surgery and documented the thyroid problem, hoping to obviate the need for an operation. Outraged that a student would attempt such a coup and fearing that he had lost his patient, the cardiac surgeon went ballistic. Threatening to have me thrown off the service, the surgeon was calmed only after the chief resident concurred with my caution, confirmed the hyperthyroid state, and later verified the normalization of the mitral valve disease once the thyroid levels had improved.

The new rules mandated that institutions finally provide private sleeping quarters for residents on night call, reflecting either the inadequacy of facilities or the disregard with which house staff was held by faculty. And more consequential still, the rules also exempted residents from drawing blood, transporting patients around the hospital, scheduling tests, and taking part in other "routine" tasks believed best delegated to others not stretched quite so thin. This interdiction stands in stark contrast to my own experience: If, for instance, I wanted a blood test for my patient,

I would write the order in the chart, retrieve the order, then draw the blood myself, take the sample down to the lab, call for the result, enter it in the chart, and write a note about it. Do these steps seem duplicative, time consuming, and ridiculous today? Indeed they do. And yet...

We now have electronic medical records for much of the paperwork, and blood-drawing teams that can access a vein and get the sample to the lab. So why would anyone attribute value to the archaic, inefficient process that once was? Today probably no one would, except perhaps to alert students to what can happen when multiple hands and multiple minds struggle to communicate—or to underscore how verbal orders may be misunderstood when rounds are not coordinated with the team around the bedside and take place instead around a computer, when everyone involved in patient care does not get to hear the plan, discuss it, and confirm consensus. Blood samples are inadvertently mislabeled, drugs are given incorrectly, and abnormal test results are overlooked. Of course, these mistakes can be made by one exhausted resident too, a risk inherent in passing a sick patient from shift to shift.

As for transportation, it makes sense on paper for an orderly to handle the transfer process, but the fact is, more than one ill patient has had a cardiac arrest en route to the ICU and failed to survive because an orderly or nurse was alone in an elevator with a sick patient. As a resident, I was never allowed to send a patient from the ward to the ICU without accompanying him or her myself.

The Paradigm Shift: A Team Approach

Accommodations made to prevent burnout were introduced after educators predicted that most inpatients would soon be cared for by full-time hospitalists. It was also assumed that hospital care would be team oriented, so patients could be handed off to others as shifts ended or fatigue set in. Many physicians, however, still choose to see their own patients on hospital rounds, are not always self-aware of their fatigue levels, are not policed to cap their patient load, and are often (and sadly) driven by enormous overhead to accept as many patients as are offered to them. Having never been exposed to such freedom during their training years, young doctors have little experience with self-regulation. In everyday practice, how does a doctor turn down a friend/patient's frantic midnight call to be seen in the ER even after having just finished pulling an all-nighter?

Acquiescence to the new practice that responsibility to one's patient ends with one's shift may hide unintended dangers. Most house staff know that the risk to patient safety peaks during shift changes. Precious time is absorbed in transferring vital data, some information may be lost, and time-sensitive treatment may be interrupted. Moreover, the "feel" for an ill patient's progress or deterioration is dulled. Familiarizing oneself with the complexity of a patient with multisystem failure is a task not always met successfully when the most knowledgeable caregiver walks away from the bedside at a pre-appointed hour. It took only a few days into my internship for me to learn this vital lesson.

I was covering the ER when several patients arrived in hemorrhagic shock from a complex motor vehicle accident: one femur protruding from the thigh, one ruptured spleen and fractured left kidney, and multiple rib fractures with a collapsed right lung. Almost simultaneously, a middle-aged woman visiting her family from the Bahamas presented with fever and a headache. My supervising resident decided to retire for the evening even though I alerted him to the woman's need to have a lumbar puncture performed to rule out meningitis. In the meantime, I spent the night furiously placing chest tubes and central lines in the three accident victims and triaging them all to their appropriate ORs.

Making the false assumption that the resident had already performed the procedure on the woman and examined her spinal fluid, I dragged myself home at the end of my exhausting thirty-six-hour shift. Still fully clothed, unable to move, and facedown in bed for fewer than ninety minutes, I was awakened by a rather frosty, cryptic call from the next shift's second-year resident demanding I return to the ER immediately to examine my patient, the Bahamian woman. Upon arrival I learned the prior resident had not left his on-call room and done as I'd asked. I was escorted to the patient's cubicle, where the new resident now cited her rapidly deteriorating symptoms of severe neck rigidity and confusion. The deferral until the morning shift in procuring her cerebrospinal fluid, which now reflected fulminant pneumococcal meningitis, he announced, had tragically delayed her treatment and altered her prognosis. He looked me in the eye and declared that my failure to assure that the procedure was completed before my shift was over would likely be responsible for her probable death.

I stood there, bone weary, stung by his proclamation, and in shock. Among my worst nightmares, I found myself implicitly labeled one of the "bad doctors." Fortunately, bolstered by high-dose antibiotics, the woman survived with only very slight permanent hearing loss in her left ear. I visited her every day on the wards until she recovered and returned to the islands. She sent me Christmas cards annually for quite some time. I used this experience in subsequent years of my residency to announce to my interns at the beginning of their rotation that any problems that took place among our patient roster was my fault alone. Their job was to learn; mine was to run interference and supervise.

The trainees of the past were encouraged (read: expected) to hand over care of a patient only after that patient's stability was ensured. This discipline would certainly be admired in their future roles as full-fledged practitioners when they refuse to leave their patient's bedside, whatever the change of shift or time of day, until the patient's condition has been clarified and improved.

I was amazed to learn from a colleague that the shift work mentality sometimes applies to current practices even in obstetrics. A woman followed during the onset of her labor by one doctor may have her baby delivered by a different obstetrician as the doctor's shift is over, functioning like a tag team to pass off the case to the next provider. In such a system, patients and their charts are considered to belong to the clinic or hospital rather than to the physician. Effectively, the doctor's proprietary interest in the case is minimized since future patients are acquired from the clinic rather than as a result of the doctor's tenacity, great care, bedside manner, or stellar reputation.

"Once this was a profession," laments my colleague, the obstetrician, "and now it is just a job."

During the months of the ravages of COVID-19, doctors and nurses waged war with a viral pandemic, armed with little ammunition and dwindling staff. It is impossible to know whether those physicians whose training included ultralong hours of work tolerated the exhaustion more easily. But at the very least, their muscle memory might have played an essential role in facilitating clinical decision-making during immense fatigue.

I asked one of my junior partners, whose own training barely preceded the institution of the ACGME rules, to give me his thoughts on teaching today's generation of students. He had a great deal to say.

"Training has changed so much. I remember long hours in the hospital, long calls, long periods at the bedside in the ICUs, the collegiality and camaraderie of suffering through ER shifts, the enthusiasm of Grand Rounds and Morning Report. Students are different now. Call today is a different animal; it is shift work. A student crafts his own curriculum, has a variety of lectures... and mandatory breaks in his day so there is no continuity in the management of patients, or consistency in being part of a medical team with attendings, fellows, residents, students, and nurses. Today's residents look like they are in a fashion show. I remember the disheveled look of a person on call struggling through the rest of his day until finally getting home to crash on the bed, only to have the alarm scream at him earlier than desired to do it all over again for another thirty-six hours."

Camaraderie and team building were the keys to survival in those wild days. On-call house staff would meet at 10:00 p.m. every night in the cafeteria, even if only for two minutes, for coffee and doughnuts provided by the hospital. We always made sure the intensive care and ER house staff, who were nailed to their stations, received their portion of sugary appreciation as well. It was a time to ask for help from the upper-level residents, to laugh, to triumph, and to catastrophize. Pagers would go off every few seconds, and everyone's hand would reflexively move to his hip, some racing off with half a glazed doughnut wad bulging from his cheek. I am guessing that doughnuts were popular at the time since kale and quinoa salad had not yet arrived on the scene.

Placing a limit on how many patients are to be followed by a given intern has its rationale during the training period when less efficient house staff are amassing experience. As with any profession, exposure to problem-solving allows trainees time to slowly grapple with which questions to ask and where to find the answers quickly. It is certainly possible that the throwing of students into an arena with too many patients jeopardizes both patient care and a student's peace of mind. Champions of the old system permitting overstuffed patient rosters endorsed this approach to training as a type of trial by fire; students encountered a wide array of diseases and became familiar with recognizing syndromes and handling complex problems. Where is the argument?

In one county hospital in Houston, the supervising attending staff went home after 3:00 p.m. until the following morning, leaving the apex of the hierarchy of expertise at the fourth-year-resident level. With adequate senior resident supervision, more junior house staff at all levels were exposed to performing or assisting with surgical procedures and clinical decisions in a way not possible in today's systems. The unfortunate result in current programs is that we graduate obstetricians and other surgeons with less experience and less self-confidence in the OR. Despite their diplomas, they still rely on senior partners (if they exist) to guide them through the more complex procedures that their predecessors had well in hand.

And yet under these pressures it is also possible that students kept making the same errors, only with simply greater efficiency. The result: supervision suffering and patient care deteriorating. Discovering the balance that offers students the chance to see every kind of disease but still have time to evaluate and incorporate best practices has been the search for the ideal.

I will simply point out that in my interrogation of most physicians trained in more recent years, I've noted how few truly vivid memories, how few "war stories" they could recall. Irrespective of its value or downside, the ACGME seems to have sanitized the medical training experience. At least one result of witnessing those terrifying or hysterical scenarios is to engrave a teaching moment with lifelong endurance.

CHAPTER 15

THE EMR BILLING PLATFORM
AND A PLEA FOR COMMON CENTS

IT IS POSSIBLE that the dilemma of our nation's healthcare costs hung far more heavily over us than I realized as a third-year medical student at UC San Diego. After all, our Medicare system was only four years old by the time I was personally responsible for spending healthcare dollars, and the program and I were both just finding our legs. For students, the issue of medical cost loomed as the least vital consideration in selecting therapies except in unusual circumstances. In 1960, healthcare in the United States accounted for only five percent of the GDP. More recently, a combination of increased use of resources by our aging population and the invention of complex diagnostic equipment and technologies, as well as the devclopment of designer biopharmaceuticals, have conspired to balloon these expenditures to 18 percent in 2020—with yet an additional four percent per year growth projected for the following three years.

To be sure, our country's demographic was different then too. In 1960, the median age in the United States was 29.5 years, but by 2019, the population's average age increased to 38.4 years—a product of a decline in birth rate and a decrease in immigration. Additionally, we now know a great deal more about the relationship between smoking and heart disease, our treatments have significantly decreased the incidence of strokes and heart attacks, and we have dramatically reduced rheumatic heart disease by more than 80 percent during the last forty years. Yet despite our increased vigilance and stricter guidelines about what we consider acceptable upper limits for blood pressure and cholesterol, the public continues to saturate itself with sugar, salt, drugs, alcohol... and ammunition. Childhood obesity is on the rise, predicting an epidemic of diabetes. Today, approximately 86 million Americans suffer from insulin resistance. We consume more resources than the rest of the world in most categories: food, electricity, oil, and yes, even healthcare. The costs keep climbing.

Testing One, Two, Three: Keeping Count of the Account

There was a time, however, during my first ward rotation in internal medicine, when my attention to issues of healthcare expenditures was directed with a laser focus by the chief. Each Wednesday morning at 9:00 a.m., the twelve third-year students on the Medicine Service would meet with Eugene the Anaconda for student-professor rounds. With the demeanor of General Patton, Eugene assembled the students in his office and fired up the troops by reminding us that this was our best chance to show him what we were really made of. His letter of recommendation for internships at the end of medical school was everything.

The Anaconda kept a master chart of every patient seen by every student on the service. Giving only thirty minutes' notice, his secretary would call one student to let them know that they would be presenting one of their patients that morning, so every student was prepared each week to give a scholarly overview of every patient they were following. And, as any feared predator would, the Anaconda was equally prepared to strike, squeeze, consume, and digest any student within range who wandered unsuspectingly into the desolate, treacherous wasteland of ignorance.

Once the name of the patient was whispered and volleyed among the queasy huddle of twelve, we had a mere twenty minutes to down some Maalox and beeline to the library to gorge on whatever information we could unearth concerning the diagnosis and therapy of the case in question. The presenter, you see, was not the only prey in the Anaconda's sight;

everyone in the room was at risk for the crushing. Sometimes the same student, bruised and still nursing his mental fang marks from the prior week, was called upon twice in a row, just to remind us that no one was safe.

The student had a companion to his misery: the intern two years his senior, who was also commanded to appear before the tribunal to confirm or refute the decisions made in the care of the patient. Thus, the intern often found himself in the proverbial "grasp of the asp," especially when it came time to justify the cost of his patient's hospital bill.

The Anaconda grilled the student to justify with reasonable plausibility why every test they'd ordered during that patient's hospital stay was medically necessary. If bloodwork, x-rays, scans, or therapies were initiated, each required a logical thread, an accounting based on rational medical science. If the student faltered, the intern was next to be interrogated. And if the chief was still unconvinced, the intern was commanded to audit the patient's entire chart and produce a detailed analysis of every expense that could not be logically explained. The total cost generated from that list was then subtracted from the patient's hospital bill—a unique handling of excessive healthcare dollars in those days... and since. Having to compensate a patient for unjustified tests at the hospital's expense was a rare and never-recurrent trauma for either student or intern. So sensitized was the house staff to enduring the wrath of the Anaconda, they learned to use extreme caution in ordering tests.

One cost- and time-saving facility, housed in a cramped corner on every ward and in ERs, was a small diagnostic lab. Consisting of a microscope, centrifuge, and other simple tools, the student was expected to obtain every patient's complete blood count; examine a urine specimen; stain a sputum or other fluid sample collected for bacteria; check blood sugars; and where appropriate, follow clotting levels. Rapid and often life-saving results could be obtained, and students became expert at diagnosis and therapy. These minilabs were removed from the wards several decades ago. While these test results currently take far longer to return when performed by the central laboratories, hospitals are now satisfied that they can levy a charge for these tests that we used to do for free. No more proverbial free lunch.

In addition to teaching us to appreciate the value of every medical dollar spent, the Anaconda was bent on pounding home the ethic and edict of accountability. No less anxiety provoking than these rounds was the ritual of the Audit Conference during my internship. At midnight every Tuesday, individual charts of a hospitalized patient other than your own were placed in each house staff's mailbox. Every intern or resident was expected to scrutinize the assigned chart in microscopic detail, complete a ten-page audit, and return it to the office. From among the roughly fifty charts, two audits were selected by the chief for their ability to highlight whose thinking had gone awry, where important clues had been overlooked, or where diagnostic findings had misled or been ignored by the team. The two cases were then presented at a conference the next day. Attendance was terrifying... and mandatory. The lesson scar lasted a lifetime.

Universal pity from colleagues invariably went out to the poor intern whose chart was being publicly skewered—along with relief that their own chart was not up for excoriation. Dodging weekly audit bullets typically required a multihour massage of every chart on every service the night before to ensure perfection and avoid the conference hot seat and the glower from the chief. Charts were buffed to a shine, patients benefitted from meticulous care, and no needle was lost in the haystack.

The deeper messages in both exercises, however, eclipsed curtailing profligate spending or attending to every feature of the chart, no matter how miniscule: It was a demand for accountability. Professors expected it, our classmates and colleagues depended on it, our patients deserved it, and we were hellbent to display it.

Why doesn't this kind of scrutiny find more traction in our current thinking, you ask? Let us peel back some of the layers.

EMR: An Epic Achievement or a Broken Record?

MUCH HAS BEEN WRITTEN about electronic medical records (EMRs). First described as a technology to track patient care in 1972 and adopted by hospitals as a way to handle a plethora of complex communications and data thereafter, EMRs found their way into private practices in the 1990s under the direction of President George W. Bush. The mandate by both Bush and President Obama to operate an electronic health record in every office posed a variety of burdens perhaps not entirely anticipated by the government, much less the public.

The practical advantages of EMR systems are fundamentally sound: They offer clarity in tracking a patient's vital signs and lab values for anemia, diabetes, high cholesterol, hypertension, kidney disease, medication use, and many other scenarios. Access to diagnostic study results is rapid and centralized, presumably obviating the need to duplicate studies that are old or lost. By alerting prescribers to a patient's allergies to medications or potentially adverse drug-drug interactions, serious complications can be avoided. Tracing the timing of prescriptions and number of pills ordered, doctors and pharmacies can determine if abuse is afoot. And an electronically ordered prescription averts the potential for error due to the illegible handwriting for which doctors are notorious. Had EMR been available thirty-five years ago, I might not have lost a patient (but not in the way you may be thinking).

A prominent older gentleman in the community was referred to me for treatment of poorly managed hypertension. Operating from the very hub of society and acting as a major force in the city's political command center, he first swashbuckled his way into my office like a James Bond impersonator, his impeccable pinstriped Brioni suit accented by a power-yellow Hermès tie that screamed machismo. After performing a careful assessment of his blood pressure needs, I gave him a written prescription for the antihypertensive beta-blocker Sectral and asked him to monitor his pressure daily and return to the office in two weeks.

The patient did return, although unannounced, in less than forty-eight hours, and furious. He recounted that the pharmacist had instead filled a prescription for Septra, after the following exchange.

"Gee, I wonder why your doctor has prescribed this medication for you?" the pharmacist had commented.

"Why do you question it?" the man had asked.

"Well, I'm used to seeing this ordered as a 'female antibiotic' for urinary tract infections," the pharmacist had replied.

Of course, the pharmacist had been mistaken on two counts: There is no such thing as a "female antibiotic," and the medication he filled instead was entirely incorrect. The patient, assuming the error was mine and perhaps taking umbrage at some subtle insult to his manhood, came to the office just long enough to toss the gender-specific pills on my desk and dramatically pivot, exiting stage left to resume his roost atop the community pedestal. Years later, I learned he had likely been fueled by his suspicion that I somehow knew about his secret, closeted lifestyle and disapproved. In a modern world of ordering medications via electronic prescriptions, this error could have been obviated and the patient may not have been lost to the practice.

As we shall see, however, no good idea goes unpunished, and EMR has its downsides. My office purchased its first EMR equipment around 2009, although the nationwide mandate to do so did not come till 2014. When first implemented, the earliest EMR systems cost solo practitioners an average of $165,000. More recently, the most widely purchased system is Epic, and its price tag can approach $1.2 million. My office sent several nurses and key business-office staff to Indianapolis for nearly two weeks to train on-site with the computer team, and upon return to act as proctors for the remaining personnel at home. During this time, the business office slowed significantly, but this deceleration was trivial compared with the effect the training had on the rest of the office. The weeks that ensued saw computer glitches, operating system crashes, vital data loss, and excruciating delays as training was disseminated throughout the office staff, nurses, and doctors.

As an incentive to comply with the mandate for such expensive equipment, the government promised the doctors a partial rebate. After many months, this promise was modified to include only those practitioners displaying "meaningful use" of the program. And then, one year later, the definition of *meaningful use* became elusive and changed more than once. In my group's experience, when only one of our fifteen doctors was too challenged by computer systems to fulfill these criteria, the reimbursement was nullified for us all.

Our nurses were warned to decrease the number of patients scheduled in the office by 50 percent. Learning how to negotiate the labyrinthine computer system was both frustrating and cumbersome. Patients waited in the office for hours to be seen and were delayed far longer to procure an appointment. While the staff's facility with the EMR systems benefitted from a definite learning curve, the constant updates and supplements demanding attention offset the savings of time we all hoped would come with familiarity, and continue to do so. The considerable reduction in time for patients to be seen has, therefore, persisted. These impediments continue to pose troublesome obstacles, since a cardiologist's patients often report complaints that cannot safely endure weeks of postponed attention. Rubbing salt on the wounds right around the same time, Medicare announced it would not reimburse more than one cardiac diagnostic test per patient visit. Some patients refused or were unable to return; others did not survive long enough to return. By multiplying the number of office visits, the pressure to accommodate patients in this environment of slowdown approached a breaking point.

EMRs do not easily speak to each other. Different system interfaces, technical challenges, cybersecurity risks, and intellectual-property concerns pose significant obstacles to seamless trans-EMR communication. The Office of the National Coordinator for Health Information Technology has proposed a plan to construct an interoperable mechanism allowing healthcare data sharing among different computer networks by 2024. Currently, a patient flown to the medical center from elsewhere still needs a paper trail rather than a computer-to-computer conversation; to encourage such techno-dialogue could be considered a HIPAA violation. For example, someone with a significant head injury diagnosed by CT scan in an outlying ER might be transported for further care to a larger hospital with only the original, local radiologist's interpretation, but often without a copy of the actual scan. The CT scan may then need repeating, since neither neurosurgeons nor radiologists can risk proceeding based on someone else's interpretation.

As mega-hospital systems began to purchase doctors' practices and compete with other independent physician groups that provide similar outpatient services, private practices feared the doctors in their referral network would be exposed by EMR-based information, then contacted and potentially lured away by the hospital-owned physicians. Accessing a practitioner's office computer system could allow hospital sleuths to potentially tap into this most valuable and jealously guarded resource, the referral network. An example of the kind of experience that fuels this paranoia was recounted to me by a cardiologist colleague on the West Coast.

He had received a call from a former research fellow asking him to see his uncle, a wealthy Italian magnate from Milan. Marcello and his wife, Donata, arrived at the highly respected destination medical center for replacement of his aortic valve. The hospital always seemed to intuit when a foreign dignitary was due to be admitted, and, as was typical, sent an Armani-suited emissary to welcome the patient and see to his comfort, while offering Donata an escort to shop at Louis Vuitton or Tiffany & Co.

When my colleague, the admitting cardiologist, first came to visit Marcello, he was surprised to find a young cardiology fellow, working with one of the competing hospital-based physician practices, already examining him. A series of orders had been written, including an internal medicine consult and a repeat of several cardiac studies already adequately performed in Milan. Outraged, my colleague banished the fellow, deleted the orders for the duplicate studies, and on the following day successfully performed Marcello's catheterization. Throughout the patient's aortic valve postoperative course, the hospital's emissary and its appointed cardiologist continued to "look in on" him surreptitiously, taking care not to write any orders or notes in the chart. During the first year following the patient's discharge, and unbeknownst to my colleague, the hospital team (including the emissary, CEO, and president of the hospital system) frequently contacted Marcello and ultimately accepted his gracious invitation to spend one week at his Lake Como villa and another at his hotel in Milan. To Marcello's chagrin, my colleague was not among the attendees; throughout this entire hospital stay, Marcello had not realized that the hospital team was a separate entity, never sent by his admitting cardiologist. While this story, and many others like it, was not facilitated by sharing between two EMR systems, it feeds the fear sensed by private-practice physicians that access by the hospital to their referring doctors' network could open opportunities for discovery by a team with whom they compete. Imagine, if you will, the reluctance of Coca-Cola to potentially expose details of its formula, employees, clients, business relationships, or marketing data by sharing a computer system with Pepsi, even if it improves operations efficiency.

Beyond the issues of privacy and intellectual property protection, our own EMR system was entirely different from that of the hospital we attended, and so additional training became necessary. Learning the new EMR protocol began with a seven-hour computer training session held at night, after office hours—an instruction that dealt only with how to discharge a patient from the hospital. Instead of completing a patient's discharge the "old way," a process that typically took twenty minutes, the newly imposed EMR system easily tripled the time.

Even after many months of experience with EMR systems, our office physicians could never ramp up the patient load to what it had been. Valuable and thoughtful as it was in theory, this computer maze exacerbated the doctor shortage. Strapped with onerous new-equipment overhead, a slowing of patient workups, declining reimbursements, and heightened competition with large hospitals, some doctors slid toward the dark side, and it became clear that the EMR could be manipulated for nefarious purposes. A subtle example of this misuse was made evident to me in recent months.

The Bill of Rights ... and Wrongs

Not long ago I was asked to review a friend's medical records since several doctors had been unable to identify the cause of his cough, fatigue, and shortness of breath. Having recovered from cardiac surgery a few months earlier, he now worried that these ongoing symptoms reflected unresolved disease, delayed complications, or perhaps a resurgent deterioration in his heart function. I agreed, and my friend sent me ninety-two pages of office notes from three consultants practicing in three separate offices. Curiously, many of the phrases used by the three doctors to describe the patient and his symptoms were suspiciously similar. In fact, the entire Review of Systems from three separate sources was *identical*, each ignoring the cough, fatigue, and shortness of breath, and each repeating the claim in the Respiratory section that the patient had no breathing complaints.

Compressing a single key on the computer had generated an entire page of fictitious (and spurious) data masquerading as a Review of Systems—an exercise that clearly had never been performed. By selecting that prompt from the pull-down menu, the chart purported to reflect the extra time taken by the doctor to ask those questions and manufactured the pretext that warranted a higher level of office visit—and hence a larger reimbursement.

Even more upsetting than the charade was the fact that the patient's chief complaints were repeatedly obscured and were perpetuated through all his subsequent charts. (An example of how this can foul things up: A nineteen-year-old patient of mine had a congenital heart problem with an EKG tracing giving the appearance that he had suffered a heart attack. Not realizing the patient's birth defect, his former cardiologist misinterpreted the tracing years earlier, and that diagnosis followed the boy in every subsequent chart, requiring incessant explanation to every future insurance company.) The obvious cause of my friend's cough and shortness of breath, had a real history been elicited, was the initiation of two drugs in his postoperative course that were well known to induce those side effects. Exchanging them for alternative medications not only resolved both symptoms, but also, had they been recognized earlier, would have averted the unnecessary expense of performing an echocardiogram, a Holter monitor, a treadmill test, an EKG, pulmonary function tests, and a CT scan!

EMRs have their foibles, but as I reflect on my experiences with student-professor rounds and Audit Conference, I now understand with greater clarity where the greatest potential pitfall actually lies: Electronic records do not hold practitioners accountable with the same oversight that the chief or one's colleagues did. The computer cannot verify whether a time-consuming Review of Systems was really performed, and does not challenge the upcharge in reimbursement associated with that fictitious task. Accountability is sacrificed for presumed efficiency. For a few, the honor system is no longer honorable. Oh, Anaconda, Horned Toad, and Iguana, where have you been hiding?

Even the most admired medical centers in the country occasionally find themselves stuck in the quicksand of dishonor. A few years ago, I was appointed to a hospital committee that explored the possibility of packaging cardiovascular services for international patients. These included complex heart surgeries like valve replacements and bypass surgery. To better understand how our hospital might stack up against other well-known medical destinations—Cleveland, Miami, Los Angeles, and Rochester—I volunteered to call these institutions posing as a physician who wanted to refer a wealthy patient from the Middle East for a procedure. Despite informing each hospital that I had already performed a precise, sophisticated cardiac catheterization (which I offered to send in advance), every hospital told me they would absolutely need to repeat every study without ever having examined the quality of my films. This was never the policy at our hospital but seemed routine at all the others. Clearly, these rules were based not on diagnostic quality control, but on financial incentives. It appeared that many hospital networks would have benefited from a refresher course in accountability.

When a Code Blue Might Only Be a Code Blew

IF YOU ARE ASKED to close your eyes and imagine a patient with pneumonia, obesity, cancer, or heart disease, you may struggle to visualize where exactly on the enormous spectrum of each of these conditions your patient is found. We all hear about patients with "walking pneumonia," not a real diagnosis, but a lay description of someone who tolerates the infection quite well. In contrast, we might easily appreciate what pneumonia might look like in septic patients with advanced bacterial or viral infections. Similarly, obesity may be mild or morbid, heart disease can reflect minimal coronary disease or end-stage heart failure, and the term "cancer" is applied to both slow-growing basal cell tumors of the skin and aggressive brain malignancies. Even within more defined categories, each diagnosis has its own life cycle, its own presenting symptoms, and its own prognosis. For this reason, the common refrain of our clinical teachers was always, "Go and see the patient."

These words are fine and useful when one doctor or student examines, evaluates, and treats one patient. As organizations responsible for paying medical bills, however, Medicare and all other healthcare insurers grapple with how to accurately position patients along this wide span of severity and prognosis. Multi-organ involvement intensifies the complexity and futility of this analysis, turning the categories into a coding nightmare much like our tax code.

The first attempt by private insurers to rein in frothy healthcare expenditures involved the development of a system called DRGs, or Diagnosis Related Groups. This initiative, introduced in 1983, featured a way to compensate hospitals and (later) physicians according to a menu of 467 diagnoses listed on the patient's hospital chart. As time went on, subcategories sprouted and ultimately burgeoned into a massive undertaking by the World Health Organization to develop a comprehensive medical classification called the International Statistical Classification of Diseases and Related Health Problems (ICD). The latest version is ICD-10, with the launch of ICD-11 offspring in January of 2022.

Aspiring to consider every detail, the developers of this coding system accepted the challenge to be as punctilious as possible. For example, an entirely different code and reimbursement applies to someone injured in a motor vehicle accident involving an inanimate object (for example, a fence) vs. a mooing (sorry, *moving*) object (for example, a cow). Sometimes the target of derision but almost by design the source of confusion, the code approaches the categorization of illness with slavish Talmudic specificity.

In real life, however, this valiant leviathan, hatched in conference rooms and think tanks around the world, can only respond to the data fed into it. Since codes and their modifiers are linked directly to the level of reimbursement, the primary goal of a hospital's coding team is to single out and apply the most catastrophic descriptors imaginable. And so every hospital and most doctors' offices have hired a Coding King or Queen, one who wields a huge and powerful financial scepter. Creative, dexterous, wily, and even devious—these are some of the essential adjectives describing the Royal Coder.

Here is an example: A patient is driven from the freeway off-ramp directly into an emergency room complaining of shortness of breath. He has a coincidental history of heart disease characterized by mild impairment of the heart muscle's ability to pump. But with a cough and low-grade fever, his predominant problem is clearly due to a viral bronchial infection. Since the upper-respiratory infection is tethered to a code with only modest reimbursement, the Royal Coder instead logs the patient into the hospital network with a primary diagnosis of congestive heart failure. The compensation to the hospital for this diagnosis is far greater. Further, since he is sent home in less than one day, the hospital is credited for taking exceptional care of heart-failure patients, most of whom might typically require treatment lasting far longer. Paid the same dollar amount for heart failure whether the patient stays for one day or twenty, the hospital celebrates a financial and reputational boon supported by the code. A steady diet of this kind of inventive coding garnishes this hospital with national recognition for its care of cardiac patients. It moves up the roster of Best Hospitals for Cardiology & Heart Surgery in *U.S. News and World Report* and becomes a destination for medical tourism. In medical school, the quest was to get the diagnosis right; today, the unholy grail is to get it paid for.

Many years ago, I suffered a medial meniscus tear of my right knee. Because the damage involved the center of the meniscus (a so-called bucket handle deformity), I required surgery rather than conservative medical management and physical therapy. This was my first surgical procedure, and though I had attended many operations, it was my first as the patient.

I slowly began to regain consciousness while being wheeled from the OR to the post-op unit. His hand on the guardrail, my internist guided the gurney briskly through the halls, hoping to arrive before my postanesthesia nausea took over. With his celebrated brand of humor, he leaned over and whispered the first words I heard after awakening from surgery:

"Milton, your orthopedist says you haven't paid him yet."

At the time, his quip was considered hilarious and repeated at dinner parties, but such comedy would turn into irony and later predict reality. Today, the sea changes of medicine seem to be roiling beneath our feet. From EMR to ICD codes, incomplete history taking to cursory physical exams, costly diagnostic and therapeutic strategies to the healthcare gap, the mechanization of clinical practice threatens the health of the art as well as the science of medicine. A colleague reminisced about the frequency with which physicians used to just pick up the phone and confer with one another. Someone in a different field always knew more, had fresh insights, and might help uncover new avenues for diagnosis and therapy. Computers seem to have replaced that interaction; the teamwork in many practices has abated. Some make the argument that our system is broken, but few inspect the root causes of the fractures, and flawed assumptions make wholesale adjustments to the system potentially ineffectual.

CHAPTER 16

THE FAULT, DEAR BRUTUS, IS NOT IN OUR HEALTHCARE SYSTEM, BUT IN OURSELVES

IN THE WINTER OF 1971, I arrived in London in my third year of medical school to begin my core rotation in pediatrics and my elective in neurology. This was my first trip abroad, and the experience was disorienting from the very start. I arrived on February 15, the very day Great Britain "went decimal." The pound sterling and shillings died a quick death. Taxi drivers, hotels, restaurants, airport personnel, and even coin-operated telephones were in disarray (none of the shillings fit in the telephone slots). Simultaneously, England had just declared a nationwide postal strike that included all communication systems, so I was unable to notify my family of my safe arrival by letter or phone for the first eight weeks of my sojourn. Fortunately, I had not yet met my future bride and, thus, was only responsible for my own survival. Within days, the weather turned forbidding and dreary, bringing bone-rattling winds from the northeast that whiplashed the city with endless sheets of freezing rain. Owning no overcoat for the first few weeks, I feared I would never again warm up or dry out.

A student from my pediatrics rotation secured a tiny room for me to rent in Blackheath, a small neighborhood in Southeast London, for four pounds sterling (about eight dollars—they still accepted sterling) per week. This austere mansion had once served as the Latvian Embassy a century before, but with its arthritic bones was ultimately abandoned as a center of Baltic diplomacy. The windows were outfitted with cracks and fissures no self-respecting window should have, and absent any noticeable heat production, the miniature radiator in my room generated little more than a rhythmic pinging noise. With its eighteen-foot ceilings, peeling gray plaster walls, and the kind of wrinkled charm that translated into no meaningful insulation, the building kept its inhabitants just marginally cozier than those asleep in the 17th-century cemetery across the street. During those first few months, life in London could, as they say, depress a hyena.

I was anxious to absorb firsthand all that I had read about London's art scene, museums, music, and culture, yet I felt hemmed in by the village-like atmosphere of Blackheath, with its one local pub and sleepy restaurant. I could hop on the bus and transfer to two different underground tube stops to venture into the city center, a journey of well over an hour, but any late-night partying in the glitzy discos around Leicester Square would require a taxi ride home. The time such an undertaking stole from my studies, as well as the squeeze on my budget, limited these forays significantly. I had borrowed $1,500 from Wells Fargo Bank before my trip, and the funds had to sustain me for six months.

My new friend from pediatrics introduced me to the South African student engineer, aspiring future barrister, and middle-school English teacher who rounded out the complement of other renters in my building. All except the teacher were born-again Christians who were rather excited to have a rabbi's son, a potential proselyte, living with them. The teacher was the only cool guy in the group, a handsome fellow who'd competed as an Olympic swimmer. He tutored me on how to comb my hair like a sophisticate, dress like I shopped in trendy Chelsea, order a "pint of Tartan" at a pub like a local, and—most important—"chat up" British women. Alas, I was far more successful as a medical student than as an athlete idol. My other housemates, unable to afford even the fifty pence for the underground subway into town and have enough left over to order a beer, subsisted on cheap steak-and-kidney pie, greasy fish and chips, or bangers and mash. True to my religious dietary restrictions, I ate just the mash, garnished with rockpiles of steamed brussels sprouts. Forty years later, their noxious scent still conjures up a most unsavory taste memory.

HOSPITALS IN THE UK: A CURE FOR WHAT *ALES* YOU

I BEGAN MY TWELVE-WEEK PEDIATRICS ROTATION at the famous Guy's Hospital, founded in 1721. Coming from the charter class at UCSD—a new school with only a young pedigree (Jonas Salk, Linus Pauling, and eight other Nobelists having arrived only after their fame was cemented)—I was in awe of Guy's and its history marked with the names of Addison, Hodgkin, and Bright (each with their own syndromes), Babington (inventor of the laryngoscope), Cooper (who discovered breast ligaments), the poet John Keats, and the scientists who coined the terms *psychedelic drugs* and *anorexia nervosa*. I soon learned, however, that the cup filled with the sagas extoling the hospital's medical achievements had runneth over years earlier and was now well diluted.

The British medical students I met there were a real departure from the American prototype. Unburdened by the thirst to keep current with the medical literature and genuinely less aggressive, whatever competitive drive they had was directed mostly toward weekend rugby. Sports and women were the predominant topics that occupied lunch, which was served in a pub in the basement of the hospital. The consumption of beer in a hospital seemed as out of place to me as the McDonalds in the lobby of the Texas Heart Institute. Many pints of Tartan ale downed by medical students at midday did not seem to interfere in any way with their intention to see patients on rounds in the afternoon! More alcohol was consumed in the pubs at noon than was used to disinfect all the hospital wards, and I, for one, was dumbfounded. On the other hand, in contrast to the students, the registrars (our resident equivalents) and professors were brilliant—and they needed to be to meet the invasion that was about to take place.

Death paid a surprise visit to London that winter, stealing a ride on the waves of the cold, dank air. Within days of my arrival, the city found itself in the grip of a massive influenza epidemic. Prioritizing the healthcare budget over its own people, London's hospitals locked their doors to new patients. I remember reading in more than one newspaper that the sad souls barred from admission who succumbed to a respiratory death were being reported as having died of natural causes. From the perspective of the healthcare budget, an out-of-hospital demise exerted the lowest overhead. During the recent coronavirus pandemic, the UK again demonstrated its approach to widespread medical battles by prioritizing resource distribution to the strong, not the weak. Ventilators used for patients who were improving but still in need of support were withdrawn from the disadvantaged to favor a younger, healthier populace, even when withdrawal might hasten the death of a patient who had been on the mend. In nonemergent times too the British healthcare system imposes strict limits of payment per person per year of "quality health." As someone who has lived in Canada and studied medicine twice in England, I have some observations on and opinions about the caution we should exert when comparing the success of other healthcare systems with that of the United States.

Critical Thinking or Just Critical?

Putting aside the array of political viewpoints, Americans seem to have accepted the media's torch song that our system of medicine is "broken." The proof of this assumption is based on several metrics: a steady and significant annual rise in the cost of healthcare delivery, large gaps in access to care for many people, poor outcomes analysis, and longevity data that lag behind the improvements reported in other Western countries. These are findings with which it is difficult to argue. But rarely has the American public been privy to the honest, base *causes* that play exacerbating roles in effecting this unsettling picture. Politicians voice their understandable concerns, even outrage, but often fail to identify some of the alternative underlying issues contributing to this apparent national disappointment.

Leveling criticism at physicians and hospitals for their poor grades may not be entirely without justification—a discussion that deserves (and will receive) some future attention. Of primary consideration, however, is the basic statistical epidemiological flaw we introduce when we try to compare entire populations of countries whose genetics, demographics, data reporting, and cultural habits are so vastly different from ours. Because it suits the agenda of the proponent, this possibly unpopular, politically incorrect discussion is almost always submerged. Pointing to our own characteristics and habits as playing a causative role in these outcomes is less attractive than blaming "the system" for our health failures.

Consider some data drawn from the World Health Organization and other fact-finding institutions to which you may not have been exposed.

In 2016, the U.S. spent roughly $9,870 per capita on healthcare compared with Japan's $4,233 and Sweden's $5,711. Outraged journalists, politicians, and public health officials love to attribute this wide discordance in spending to our greater number per capita of MRI and CT scanners, yet despite these advantages, we are experiencing a decrease in life expectancy... as if this correlation has any validity. The fact is, we are a different people than the Japanese and the Swedes—and any other population, for that matter.

Would It Kill You?

Let's start with the matter of obesity: The prevalence of this condition in the United States exceeds 36 percent of the population, compared with 4.3 percent among the Japanese. As an admittedly extreme but not altogether unique example, in my senior year I was assigned a patient who weighed well over 700 pounds. She was measured on the meat scales in the basement of the hospital, and two beds were lashed together to accommodate her bulk. Her guilty pleasure involved consuming large pots of buttered noodles prepared for her by her devoted, 145-pound husband. The pots were conveniently stashed under her bed at home for easy access. Tragically, her ability to aerate her lungs was thwarted by the massive weight of her chest. For her, each breath was like lifting an anvil, and despite heroic resuscitative efforts, she died of respiratory failure.

Alerted to the far-reaching problem of obesity in the United States, I would often sit at a coffee shop or in the ER waiting area, just checking out the bodies. It became clear to me that I would soon be dealing with both genetic and dietary problems that would seriously complicate caring for this high-risk group and affect their life expectancy, especially when compared with what was found in other First World countries.

Approximately 11 percent of Americans aged twenty to seventy-nine are diabetic, while only four percent of Swedes are similarly afflicted. Fewer American males are found to engage in sufficient exercise compared with Swedish males. Moreover, the parameters conventionally used to measure cardiac risk factors—high blood pressure, smoking, diabetes, high cholesterol—fail to fully account for the pivotal genetic differences seen in the populations of entire countries.

But there are even more differentiating factors at play. In the first four months of 2021, 160 mass shootings were reported in the United States. During my month-long student rotation in the emergency room in San Diego in 1970, I had no fewer than three episodes in which a gun was pointed at me. As an intern in the ER at Denver General Hospital (one of eight other facilities being showcased in a television documentary film on violence in America), I noted an even greater prevalence of guns. This stood in sharp contrast with my experience in the ERs of London and underscores the additional challenges faced by American physicians compared with their counterparts. *Violent death meted out on the streets cannot be attributable to poor doctoring.* Gun violence in the United States kills 4.43 victims per 100,000 people. This number supersedes that reported for Afghanistan (3.96), Iraq (3.54), and Syria (0.99). In fairness, records kept in those countries undoubtedly suffer from inaccuracies, since deaths from the off-loading of military weapons may have been excluded from these statistics and categorized separately. Nevertheless, that any Western democracy can be included as a member of this unique club of tinderboxes is a tragedy. In contrast, guns in Japan are responsible for only 0.04 victims per 100,000 (1/100 of the US).

Opioid addiction claims many lives and even more healthcare dollars. In 2015, American patients received one dose of an opiate for every 20 patients; the rate in Japan was one dose for every 800 patients. As a result, drug overdoses in the US increased 255 percent from 1999 to 2017. In 2016, opioid addiction afflicted 1.04 percent of Americans, more than ten times the number seen in Sweden. But even before opiates became so fashionable, I attended to many dozens of overdosing patients who were rescued from trash-bins, the backseats of rusted-out pickup trucks, Saturday night raves in Balboa Park, and high-rise executive suites. My classmates all quickly learned to recognize the telltale signs of heroin overdose—pinpoint pupils and even, occasionally, scalded skin around the rectum, the result of a prevalent but false belief that pouring boiling coffee into the rectum of a comatose heroin addict would be lifesaving. Outraged, and regardless of the hour, I made it a ritual to personally call the psychiatrists who prescribed large quantities of designer psychoactive drugs with reckless abandon. And if I woke them up in the middle of the night, so much the better.

Motor vehicle accidents have steadily declined in the US and throughout the world, doubtless thanks to standard safety features built into new cars. The improvement in the US, however, has lagged behind that seen in other Western countries. Why? We still lose 10.3 people per 100,000 (regrettably leading the world) compared with the Japanese at four per 100,000, and even fewer in Sweden. One reason: Tragically, eighteen out of twenty transportation-related deaths are associated with Americans' failure to wear a front-row seatbelt. The remaining explanation for America's high motor-vehicle fatality is due to the much longer driving distances we log compared with those undertaken in Europe or Asia. Are these tragedies a result of the broken healthcare system? Perhaps. Or are they impacted by the personal choices we make, by America's insistence on shrugging off rules, a mindset that may spawn creativity but also shaves years off our average life span?

IT'S THE LITTLE THINGS THAT MEAN SO MUCH

ANOTHER SIGNIFICANT CONTRIBUTOR to the disappointing life expectancy ratings for the United States, and certainly a chronic criticism of the quality of American medical institutions, is the tragic case of infant mortality. Defined as the number of deaths within the first year of life per 1,000 live births, the highest mortality statistic in the world is in Afghanistan, at 110.6, while the lowest is in Monaco, at 1.8. The data for the United States, however, is hardly encouraging. The World Health Organization report describing our infant mortality rate of 5.8, compared with Japan's 2.0 and Sweden's 2.6, is both wrenching and inexplicable. No single contributor to our comparably diminished longevity has more of a devastating impact than averaging in the death of a newborn. Why does the United States do so poorly, and is this yet another example of a tarnished record of healthcare delivery and the welfare gap? Let us take a closer look.

The greatest factors responsible for the high infant mortality in America come from congenital abnormalities associated with stillbirths, and approximately 40 percent are derived from sudden infant death syndrome (SIDS). Neither of these elements necessarily implies inferior healthcare, but they do relate to several known risks. Compared with their European and Asian counterparts, American women have the highest percentage of pregnant mothers under age twenty (roughly seven times greater than seen in Sweden or Japan). Maternal obesity, smoking history, and drug use during pregnancy—essentially a continuation of my earlier discussions—are thought to play major roles in causing congenital defects, preterm birth, and low birthweight. Educating new mothers about preferred sleeping positions and conditions for infants is a vital feature of preventing SIDS but is not available to all. Many studies have questioned how many of these issues around infant deaths are related to genetic predispositions to congenital defects or to maternal education, prenatal care, overcrowding, or diet. Poor and underserved inner-city communities, as well as rural and remote populations, experience impaired access to quality information and healthcare. And even in situations where care is offered for free, many mothers refuse to take advantage of those services out of fear. Conspiracy theories abound, rumors ruminate, and infant survival suffers.

During my month-long OB-GYN rotation at the large County/University Hospital in San Diego, just a few miles north of Tijuana, I attended any number of women who were desperate to deliver their babies on US soil so they could be counted as American citizens. Many whose prenatal care had been displaced by the subsistence needs of the rest of the family waited just across the border until their contractions were minutes apart. Nearly scooping them off the steps of the hospital, I delivered more than three dozen infants that month, and these high-risk deliveries and their anticipated complications were folded into the statistics of the American medical system. As a third-year student, I would not typically have been allowed to deliver twins, but I did on two occasions, since the Mexican mother was unaware and wholly unprepared during her pregnancy for her surprise packages.

Some less than obvious components, however, should also be addressed. Perinatal mortality, frequently considered to be the best indicator of the quality of medical care, is comparable if not better in the United States than in its European counterparts. Further, the often more aggressive CPR interventions employed by American obstetricians during the first moments of birth (even in infants with poor outcome expectations) contribute to how infant mortality is tabulated. Different from American classification, reports from European and Asian countries regarding the birth of "nonviable" fetuses weighing less than 500 grams excludes them from being labeled as infants. This distinction in definition is thought to contribute up to 30 percent of the gap between American infant mortality statistics and those from elsewhere.

The United Fates of America

AT LEAST TWO-THIRDS OF THE GAP in life expectancy between the United States and other Western countries is due to mortality rates for people under age fifty. The major contributors, excluding recent COVID-19 data, are infant mortality, transportation, cardiovascular disease, homicide, and drug overdose. We would not think of impugning the clinical expertise of Asian gastroenterologists because 60 patients per 100,000 Koreans, 32/100,000 Japanese, but only 4.7/100,000 Americans suffer from gastric cancer. These statistics do not imply a failure of their medical system, but rather a function of genetics and diet. Nor should we target American medicine for lack of success in treating deaths from homicide, drug overdose, or automobile accidents. We are a diverse population, with different diets, risk factors, genetic predilections, cultural norms, and needs. We should not ignore, however, the disarticulated relationship between American medicine and our treatment of mental illness and the highly significant risk that psychiatric dysfunction imposes on some of these factors.

It is too simplistic to address these difficult comparisons by demanding that Americans become a renovated people. We are not going to think and act and eat like the Japanese, be as svelte as the Italians, exercise like the Swedes, or drive like the Swiss. Our entrepreneurial spirit, unique attitudes, and concern about the usurpation of our individual rights impair the communal solidarity of our healthcare decisions. No better example of the negative impact of this characteristic was seen in the way Americans chose to address the challenges of COVID-19. Was our country's relatively dismal performance during the pre-vaccine year of the pandemic an example of a broken medical system; overcrowded living conditions for much of our high-risk population; a lack of foresight to plot a national algorithm for triage, testing, and delivery of equipment; or the renegade mindset of a population refusing to adhere to medical advice? Or perhaps it was all the above.

We have offered the American dream as a goal to pursue in our quest for happiness, not as a promise to own the treasure map to success. Many would propose that a significant operant in our healthcare problems is the wealth gap in the United States. Undoubtedly this is so, and without question it is a major contributor that deserves serious consideration. Access to care is far from uniform and not guaranteed. But mending the healthcare system by introducing sweeping policy changes proven to be solutions for other countries may either apply the wrong cure for the wrong disease or may be insufficient in overcoming even more important issues.

Certainly, we have already hinted at changes with which most would not find fault. Going back to the habit of taking a verifiable history and performing a thorough exam will help doctors direct resources to the right illness. Consulting with radiologists and nuclear-medicine physicians to optimize our choices of diagnostic studies should decrease ordering duplicative tests. Some studies have shown that seeing a specialist first helps to identify the fastest (and therefore least expensive) way through the maze. Remembering the lessons of professor-student rounds by ordering a test only if there is a rational, defensible reason for it will save time and money as well. Encouraging an aura of accountability in this era of computing may require training programs and innovative software to reinvigorate an emphasis on medical ethics.

Hoping for an instant remedy for our rampant obesity, Americans flock to fad diets, surgical interventions, and dietary supplements. Legitimate, evidence-based studies can certainly provide sound advice regarding dietary indiscretion, but these approaches require time and dedication. The public would be better educated if the FDA demanded simpler product labeling that does not permit marketers to obscure the real nature of its ingredients. Students should be taught in school what it means to be organic, GMO, low-fat, protein-rich, vegan, heart-healthy, low-salt, biodynamic, and sustainable. They must learn to read about, and better understand, what they have purchased and are about to consume.

Some propose we roll back healthcare costs to those spent in the 1960s, which would be possible only if we eliminated any of the costly innovations that have been developed or invented since then—by which we mean expensive but life-saving immunotherapy for cancer, coronary bypass surgery, genetic testing, stent insertions, and brilliant imaging technologies—like MRIs, CT scans, and 3-D ultrasounds—that save countless lives. But there are other far more plausible ways to stretch the healthcare dollar.

THE DRUG LORDS

IT IS TRUE THAT WE HAVE some of the highest drug costs in the world. In 2016 we spent $1,011 on drugs per capita compared with Sweden's $351—the lowest among Western countries. Why the difference? At least one answer is that the US spends enormous amounts in drug development. Recent estimates suggest it costs $4 billion to bring a drug successfully to market. The price tag takes into consideration that only 1 in 5,000 experimental drugs reaches the threshold of success. But are there ways to shrink that expense without jeopardizing curative innovation?

In 2017, the United States spent $71.4 billion on research and development, but it also spent $5.9 billion on direct-to-consumer advertising, mostly on TV. In fact, the US is joined only by New Zealand in this kind of campaign, which doing the math represents eight percent of the R&D overhead yet offers no useful information to doctors or patients. Additional expenditures include employing the big-pharma lobby, which peaked in 2020 at $220 million.

To a large extent, the least controllable portion of the cost to bring a drug to market comes in the last phases of human trial; of all pharmaceuticals studies that finally reach the ultimate Phase 3 trials, only fourteen percent are eventually released to market. One biotech company has begun work on developing 3-D printing of human liver and kidney tissue to address this because when experimental drugs are investigated, they most often fail clinical trials due to adverse effects on one of these organs, by which time an enormous investment in time and money has already taken place. One day, 3-D printed organs may allow biopharmaceutical companies to discard potentially toxic experimental drugs much earlier in their development by verifying their adverse effects on human tissue before discovering these issues during later, more expensive clinical human studies. Of course, these research models may mimic the structure of liver cells and tissue, but do not reflect the biochemistry of these organs—perhaps failing to achieve the sensitivity needed to accurately imitate the impact of these drugs on human organs. Rapid acquisition of genetic sequences jump-started the quest for COVID-19 vaccine production in record time. Designer drugs based on messenger RNA and gene-editing technology promise a faster, more targeted generation of medicines with a higher likelihood of success—one benefit emerging from the desperation of the pandemic.

Economies of Scale Can Tip in Either Direction

IN A SINCERE EFFORT to ensure healthcare delivery to all Americans, a variety of proposals have been offered by politicians, one popular version of which is Medicare for All. Most physicians would agree that having a single payer could potentially unclutter the cumbersome, duplicative, and expensive morass of payers. And yet consider our ICD-11 coding system, our tax code, and our Veterans Health Administration hospital system: Despite the adage supporting economy of scale, bigger is not always better or more efficient. Far less frequently addressed by its cheerleaders are a few of the unintended consequences of Medicare for All. But before diving into that discussion, I offer details from my own personal experience.

Roughly twenty-five years ago, my cardiology group of six decided to build a private cardiac catheterization laboratory, believing we could provide a better service in a more tranquil environment at a lower cost. As its first director, I agreed to partner with our hospital if their input was kept at arm's length, leaving construction and management entirely in our hands. At about the same time, the hospital was preparing to update the equipment in one of their own ten cath lab suites—a project that was limited to replacing one aging camera and some software for some newer technology. In comparison, we planned to build two lead-lined rooms, a film-viewing room, eight patient beds for pre- and post-procedure examinations, a radiology processing lab, a kitchen, two offices, a specialized ventilation system, safety inspection permits, and an entirely independent emergency generator. Although both projects began almost simultaneously, our lab was built for half the cost, in one-third of the time of the hospital's. Our success was dependent on the cooperative efforts and practical suggestions of our six experienced cardiologists and the insightful guidance of our highly qualified executive director.

Before opening our lab, we introduced procedures to avoid waste. We carefully selected catheters, judiciously used expensive contrast dye, enforced efficient scheduling, limited radiation exposure, and maintained an environment of heightened safety. Our complications rate was one-ninth that of the national average for the first 14,000 patients we served. Going beyond the norm, we even invited the Joint Commission on Accreditation of Hospitals to evaluate our facility using the same standards they would demand of fully functioning hospitals. In the first few years, we were able to perform the same catheterization technique as the hospital's but for one-tenth of the cost and eight times the profit margin. Compared with the hospital, a comparable savings was enjoyed in our office charges for ultrasound, treadmill, nuclear, and Holter monitor studies.

Over the ensuing twenty years, as our patient population aged and Medicare became the major payer, our profit margins shrank. In time, the cost to perform a catheterization exceeded the reimbursement, resulting in the lab's dissolution. Patients then had to be referred to the hospital's facilities, where costs to Medicare and third-party insurers remained many orders of magnitude greater.

Politicians seem afraid or unwilling to address the serious possibility that if all hospitals were to depend on Medicare reimbursement for their entire revenue, many less robust facilities would fail. Often, the small buffer between survival and bankruptcy for hospitals is provided by private insurance payers. Decreasing reimbursement to Medicare levels for all patients—the lowest common denominator—could extinguish any profit margin, leaving much of rural America without access to a nearby hospital. Patients becoming ill will then attempt to access major medical centers, but even the larger hospitals will be on "drive by" as capacity is overrun. Such was the case during the Clinton era, in which public health experts proposed "right-sizing" (a euphemism for downsizing) hospital bed capacity, resulting in a huge layoff of nurses and closing of wards. They believed that by encouraging healthier lifestyles and supporting trends toward outpatient, rather than in-hospital care, fewer facilities would be needed and costs could be contained. They soon came to understand that a policy voted on in a boardroom is not always reflected in a shift in the habits of a nation. And by the time the experiment was recognized as having failed, wards could not be reopened, since nurses were no longer available for staffing.

In a Medicare for All system, issuing an insurance card to every American might not translate into Medicare *access* for every citizen. We can compare universal healthcare delivery with our closest cousin, Canada, noting at the surface that Americans pay $2,497 per year for administrative costs, while Canadians pay only $580 (administrative costs are 31 percent of health dollars in the US vs. 17 percent in Canada). Canadians would seem to have tapped into a bargain until one considers the 57 percent income tax for people earning $292,000 per year (36–51 percent higher than in the US), for which $39,000 is devoted to healthcare.

There is yet another hidden expense associated with waiting for care. More than the obvious risk of delaying treatment of heart disease or the toll extorted by the progression of cancer, the Canadians' logjam costs them $5.8 billion in lost wages. Patients in need of hip, shoulder, or knee replacements cannot do manual labor. Neither can a worker function with severe back pain. Employers, too, fear liability if they endanger employees awaiting heart surgery, treatment for epilepsy, or cancer chemotherapy by insisting they continue on the job. Canadians wait an average of 39 weeks to see an orthopedist, 10.6 weeks to get an MRI, and 20 weeks for coronary bypass surgery. The worst delays exist in the province of New Brunswick, where average wait time to be seen for a specialty referral exceeds 45 weeks, and neurosurgery is postponed for 26 weeks. Most brain tumors refuse to wait that long.

The Canadian healthcare system that some in the US hope to emulate forces 63,000 patients per year (out of a population of only 35 million) to seek more timely treatment in the United States. Were we to adopt the Canadian approach, could we justifiably predict the same delays would take place in the United States? I do not know—but it is because I do not know, because unintended consequences are possible, that incremental adjustments, like adopting a single-payer system and overhauling the pharmaceutical industry, make more sense.

CHAPTER 17

IT SERVES YOU RIGHT

Early one spring morning a young man walks briskly by a pond in the park on his way to his swimming team trials for the summer Olympics. No one could fault him for being anxious, but he does risk disqualification for running late. After all, he has trained for this day for a decade or more and circled the date nearly four years before. As he rounds the corner, the athlete hears a splash and a gasp. Thrashing frantically in the water is a four-year-old boy who has eluded the watchful eye of his nanny, escaped into the lake, and is about to submerge for the last time. Does anyone question what happens next? Is there a difficult decision to be made? What action must the athlete take to do the right thing?

Natural law dictates that we respond in certain ways, neither for personal gain nor to avoid public retribution but simply because we ought to do so. In his *Critique of Pure Reason*, the 18th-century German philosopher Immanuel Kant proposes that we cannot fully know ourselves, the whole world, the soul, or God; we can only understand ourselves via our moral choices. He defines this ethical roadmap as "transcendental idealism," a universal respect for humanity. According to Kant, we can appreciate the natural, observable world only by absorbing what we experience and using that information to influence how we must act—Kant's "categorical imperative." The athlete's moral self senses an obligation and responds to the natural law of saving a life. The choice is not weighed or measured; there is no accounting, it is immediate and instinctual. Kant writes, "Morality is not properly the doctrine of how we make ourselves happy, but how we make ourselves worthy of happiness."

Apart from anticipating the consequences of our misdeeds or our failing to act morally, our free will moves us to do what we ought to do. Predestination sidelines our free will and absolves us from the outcomes of our poor choices. Rising to the challenges of 9/11, Hurricane Harvey, or World War II, heroes did not step up to collect awards or headlines. During the pandemic of 2020, caregivers rushed to save the metaphorical drowning boy in the pond and the dying citizens of the world, using the instincts that make them human and the skills they honed from years of training and sacrifice. And the imperative to act without question was never more on display than during the coronavirus plague. Nurses, doctors, teachers, police, and grocers chose to perform their duties, functioning to keep life going despite the woeful absence of equipment for their own personal protection.

"It's what we do," said Mary, a millennial family practitioner in New York City, matter-of-factly. She and so many of her colleagues raced against time to provide medical services to hospitalized patients, contracted COVID-19 themselves, and returned to the battleground for another round. Terrified family members learned to accept or subjugate their fears concerning the welfare of the heroes they loved.

For the first responders who battle a blazing building, disperse a mass riot, contain a deadly contagion, rescue the stranded from a category-five hurricane, or protect us from an assault on our nation, the prospect of heroism plays no role. To do what one must is simply a call to advocate for what is perceived to be a natural law, a categorical imperative.

Category 4-F: A Moral Imperative

I WOULD NEVER CATEGORIZE my tagging along with the Flying Samaritans to open weekend clinics in the Chihuahuan Desert in my first years in medical school as a response to the call of a natural law. The choice I made was an easy one; I had by far the most to gain. Anxious to dip my toe into the pool of indigent clinical medicine, I saw my time spent in rural Mexico not as a sacrifice, but as a unique opportunity. This was to be the inauguration of my clinical experience.

The same could be said about one of the obvious choices we later made as third-year students. As members of the only medical school within a 100-mile radius, my classmates and I quickly perceived the challenges imposed on the community because of the uneven access to healthcare in rural California. In response to that void, we began working in a free clinic in Imperial Valley. As the news of the clinic spread rapidly, we were inundated with patients ensnared by drug addiction, socially transmitted diseases, unwanted pregnancies, malnutrition, and spousal abuse.

A significant number came for their induction physicals for the armed forces. These were mostly scared young men, some of whom sensed they were purchasing a one-way ticket to the Far East. We students were immune from this outcome; the temporary shelter from the dangers of Vietnam afforded us by enrolment in medical school stood in glaring contrast to the boys we examined. My visceral reaction to the war and the expressions of terror etched on the faces of these young inductees was one of vicarious pain. One patient developed psychological blindness for six months, describing how he visualized with his "third eye" a nightly foray into the jungle that ended as he dipped his hand into a pool of Asian blood and wiped it on a banana leaf; another spent weeks jumping off his family's piano in a failed attempt to develop flat feet—both boys desperate to avoid the alternative, open-ended separation from family by escape to Canada. I also remember one breathless, pudgy, still-closeted young fellow who entertained macabre visions predicting either his death by sniper or humiliation by homophobia. I used what wiles I could to find exit strategies for them, mindful that discovery by authorities could remove me from being of help to anyone. Some I pronounced 4-F by having them surreptitiously consume large quantities of licorice—the glycyrrhizic acid component, undetectable by assay, inducing temporary hypertension. We came to appreciate with increasing clarity how challenging life could be for some people our age. For those of us who came from living mostly privileged lives, this was a chance to better understand and serve the broader spectrum of humanity in our midst, not so much a natural law, but more of a Darwinian law of natural selection. Many young lives in jeopardy, too many lost.

If the medical world seems a little more callous, a little less personal, and a little more removed from the kind of intimacy that a doctor-patient relationship used to imply, perhaps technology and medical training have been the unintended culprits. The pressures of time give way to speed and efficiency, while warmth and confidence cede their importance to accuracy in diagnosis and treatment. Not at all a bad tradeoff... unless we demand that our patients deserve both. I had to wait until I retired to observe a resurrection of the natural law of service as it must have been played out decades ago in rural environments. I am talking about my tangential experience with healthcare delivery in sub-Saharan Africa, a throwback to the medicine of yesteryear.

Long-Distance Calling

After I retired, I considered how I might renew that commitment to service that had compelled me in the past and beckoned anew. On a vacation to Southeast Asia, my wife and I were befriended by a remarkable woman whose local priest was one of the cofounders of the Touch Foundation, a faith-based ministry that supported a large hospital and launched a medical school in Mwanza, Tanzania. Within a few days, I was contacted by the CEO of the Weill Bugando Medical Center and invited to visit the facility. I was on a nineteen-hour flight a few months later.

In the days leading up to my travels, I prepared by spraying my clothing with permethrin to discourage attacks from mosquitoes and began my trial of antimalarial medication. The moderate nausea and nightmares the meds first introduced ultimately faded, as did the soreness from hepatitis and typhoid shots. While yellow fever was not an immediate problem, the threat of dengue fever and an abundance of lesser-known vectors was always top of mind.

The Houston-Frankfurt-Dar Es Salam-Arusha legs of the trip were long yet straightforward, but the last flight on a little puddle jumper kicked off the reality show. Arriving in Mwanza near the southernmost border of Lake Victoria, I could never have envisioned the enormity of the challenges of medical practice in this Third World environment.

Appreciating the risks of kidnapping or theft inherent in hailing a random taxi at the airport in this city of nearly three million, the medical center sent Nyanda to collect me and to be my personal driver for the next ten days. We became fast friends, he with a thirst to improve his English, read books, and study American ways, and I with a need to understand the Tanzanian mindset. We talked about life in his village and the challenges he bravely faced in dealing with his only child's inoperable congenital heart defect.

I had come to the Weill Bugando Medical Center to identify the gaping holes in the hospital's function. Nyanda warned that my natural tendency to diagnose a problem, jump in, and fix it would be met with distrust, and was not the typical African approach. Nyanda was unusually open, an anomaly by African standards. In a world stained by colonialism, most Western-Black relationships tiptoed on cautious feet. The enduring part of the occasional success story rarely unfolded before the second or third act of the ballet. When he dropped me off to freshen up, my driver was pleased to see I had been billeted in the best hotel in town.

The Hotel Tilapia was named after one of the only fish able to survive the horribly polluted waters of Lake Victoria. As bottom-feeders living in a nutritionally depleted environment, tilapia have acquired a taste for the copious animal "poop" defiling the lake. In a triumph over the freshwater parasite that penetrates even unbroken skin and causes a disease called schistosomiasis, the fish have found a way to deflect the toxins produced by the GI and bladder infections that have killed everything else in the lake. As I opened the door to my hotel bedroom, I understood how the owners arrived at the name. Checking the mosquito net for holes and seeing none, however, afforded me a minute of gratitude for small favors. Looking skyward, and in the low-wattage light from the single dangling bulb, I could barely make out the characteristics of the vibrant fauna scurrying around the ceiling. I was already anxious to test the tensile integrity of the netting and reconsidered sampling the tilapia special on the menu. Served with a side of fried plantains, rice, vegetables, and "secret sauce," the fish was edible as long as I ignored its provenance. Even the fishermen cautiously avoided direct contact with the lake water due to the potential for infection through even unbroken skin—a fear combining elements of *Jaws* and a sinister plot from *Heart of Darkness*.

Jet-lagged and disoriented, I awoke the next morning, got dressed on my bed while still protected by the mosquito net, and dashed downstairs to the lobby, where Nyanda met me with a knowing smile and a lifesaving cup of robust Tanzanian coffee. After a short drive he dropped me off at the front gate of a large edifice thronged by an animated crowd chattering in a riot of dialects channeling the Tower of Babel and dressed in a rainbow of colors and uniforms representing the 120 different tribes in the country. After a most uncomfortable, nonverbal face-to-face stare-down that lasted for minutes, the intimidating and rather enormous ebony guard was persuaded by a hospital emissary to let me enter the walled compound.

This trip to Mwanza was designed for me to provide an in-depth needs analysis of the hospital during a nearly two-week period. I felt as though I was looking through a keyhole into a century-old healthcare infrastructure in which the basic prospects of clean water, dependable electricity, functioning equipment, and pharmaceutical availability were not givens. And at the heart of this 960-bed facility was a group of nurses and physicians whose personal sacrifice may have been prompted by their faith but whose dedication was a manifestation of their moral self—the natural law of providing service simply because one ought to do so.

The hospital, built between 1968 and 1977 by the Catholic Church, still looks like the concrete pillboxes one imagines pockmarking the Maginot Line. The young medical school is partially supported by the Weill Cornell Medical College, which provides funds and sends about forty residents to rotate for a short time through the wards. A few faculty members from Cornell also teach for brief periods, but the chairs of the departments of surgery, medicine, and pediatrics are mostly Americans who trained at premier medical centers in the US, brilliant teachers whose dedication moves them to trade international academic recognition for the incremental changes to best practices they can promote in relative obscurity. Their inspirational efforts are frequently undermined by circumstances that would upend most practical thinkers who function most efficiently in a system driven by a meritocracy.

The many personal shortcomings I have lamented about in American medicine—reliance on technology, computer-assisted history taking, cursory physical exams, the abandonment of touch—still have a place here. But in Tanzania, cultural mores can play havoc with progress. Years of colonialism have stiffened the native resolve against change and have undermined a drive to self-improvement. An innate suspicion of foreign intervention and absence of faith in the promises of outsiders have delayed, if not poisoned, any good intentions toward the betterment of a flawed system. The hospital's water supply is contaminated with Klebsiella bacteria that saturates the walls of the neonatal intensive care unit and causes severe pulmonary infections. Ninety percent of newborns and their mothers who are called to supplement the inadequate nursing care become ill. Much of the equipment donated from hospitals from around the world arrives already broken or eventually succumbs to the punishment of a harsh sub-Saharan climate. Qualified biomedical engineers are hard to find, and replacement parts for medical equipment constructed in different countries are expensive to import. As a result, most of that equipment lies fallow. Reagents needed as components for vital blood tests are delivered to the hospital inconsistently and at the whim of a supplier, imperiling patients who must undergo urgent surgery. The absence of electronic charting, intensive-care nurses, quality management committee oversight, teaching conferences, or even in-house code-blue teams would paralyze most American physicians and nurses and dissuade many from entering the fray. I had hopes that the $300,000 placed in my care by a former patient wishing to support my humanitarian efforts, buoyed by matching funds from USAID to Africa and grants from various drug companies ($1 million in all), might make a dent in addressing these deficits. These obstacles seem insurmountable.

And yet... they arrive, and they remain. A young Tanzanian physician spends five years training in Holon, Israel (a free program offered to Third World specialists) to become the only cardiac surgeon in Tanzania, but he must learn to negotiate the skepticism and placate the obstinacy of the old guard who commit malpractice with stunning regularity by refusing to change their outdated methods. A single female pediatric cardiologist/intensivist from Germany comes for a few months and stays for seven years. As a Caucasian woman hoping to thrive in an environment whose seared memory of Tanzania under both German and British control can turn unpredictably hostile, she senses her mobile life around Mwanza is occasionally threatened and stifling. Declining more attractive career offers to transfer back to Germany, she can be seen every morning in an unpainted gray concrete room performing cardiac ultrasound tests on glassy-eyed Maasai babies, their frail whimpers silenced by bobbing a colorful bird feather from a string, their favorite—and only—toy.

The talented chief of surgery is a woman whose credentials include an undergraduate degree from Case Western Reserve, medical school at Emory, two master's degrees in healthcare quality and public health from Northwestern, and a former medical school faculty position at the University of North Carolina School of Medicine. Her eight years in Tanzania was preceded by work in Uganda. Her office, three blocks from the hospital, is surrounded by the most robust small businesses within that radius: coffin makers for children. Living thousands of miles from her extended family, she serves at the command of her moral self.

SOME GOOD DEEDS DO GO UNPUNISHED

AS DISCUSSED IN THE TALMUD, the reward for doing a *mitzvah*, a good deed, is the mitzvah itself. Our unsung, unrewarded, unexpected actions do not have to save a limb or a life or a soul, nor do they even have to be noticed for them to be considered a mitzvah. But just for the record, here are a few of the minor innovations introduced in Africa recently that eventually did have a huge impact.

In the jungle, many pregnant women suffer from anemia related to their meager diet and lack of prenatal vitamins. They give birth to underweight infants who are often premature and who, in the absence of ventilators, have a dismal chance of survival. Teams of healthcare workers venture into the rugged terrain to identify those at risk by using a simple mechanical "salad dryer" centrifuge that spins down a drop of blood to measure the red-blood-cell count. Once recognized, the anemic expectant mother is given a necklace strung with multiple doses of iron supplements cleverly pressed into the shape of a fish. The mother, who might otherwise have been skeptical about accepting pills from an outsider, instead is encouraged to swallow a "lucky fish" from her necklace each day. Her iron deficiency resolves, and her baby survives.

In some villages, rudimentary thatched neonatal wards in the jungle accommodate scores of newborns. Tragically, frayed wires, faulty circuitry, and the sputtering motors from aging equipment occasionally spit out an electrical spark that erupts into a prison of flames. Until recently, nurses could grab only one infant in each arm to carry them to safety, the rest succumbing to a fiery death. Then one inventive nurse designed a new apron with fifteen large pockets sewn onto the entire front panel, which is currently worn by all nurses. Now when a spontaneous fire threatens to consume the ward, each nurse can save fifteen babies at a time.

In Ghana, inhabitants assume the same last name of their village, so that recording their medical histories, following epidemics, and tracking their medication regimen become a nightmare. A handheld iris detection system the size of a computer mouse is brought into the villages and connects remotely to a central computer in the medical center. Patients are thus identified biometrically, and early recognition of an outbreak of infection allows officials to impose measures of quarantine that quell transmittal more rapidly.

With the tenacity that demands decades of persistence to bear sustainable fruit, those who serve quietly follow a natural law. In contrast to the last words from John Milton's poem "On His Blindness," "They also serve who only stand and wait," the valiant at the Weill Bugando Medical Center stand and serve... but refuse to wait.

CHAPTER 18

HOW TO CHANGE YOUR MIND

MOST FIRST-YEAR MEDICAL SCHOOL COURSES favor the student with the best memory. Anatomy, physiology, biochemistry, cell biology, and pathology all rely heavily on one's ability to absorb huge boluses of information to be stored for later practical application. In that regard, the champions of rote, capable of spewing encyclopedic lists of facts, tend to rise to the head of the class. Many of my own classmates came to school with advanced degrees in other fields and consequently were removed from rote learning, having spent their most recent years thinking deep thoughts. As a result, their true brilliance was sometimes less on display at the beginning but became more obvious as time went on. Especially as the computer era matured, acquiring data became less of a hurdle than appreciating what question to ask. Thus, after our first few years of study, we began the necessary transition from rote to deductive reasoning, an evolution that terrorized some and was applauded by others.

Wild Speculation

SOMETIMES THE STUDENTS WITH the deepest well of facts in the first two years may soon be revealed as having the shallowest insight. Consider this classic example recounted by a colleague: It's likely that young Roger's stellar undergraduate grades at UCLA were carried on the back of a photographic memory. But his fundamental understanding of the mechanisms of health and disease were both the least rational and the least practical, and his dearth of common sense when functioning in unfamiliar clinical territory was painfully conspicuous.

Physicians have all circulated apocryphal war stories like the dandy about the Appalachian woman who comes to the emergency room having noticed "leaves in my Virginia," and who had somehow in the past few weeks misplaced an avocado pit in her "Netherlands." But although there may be a few other embellished stories about Roger, this one is by far the most outlandish, the one too absurd to have been manufactured, and the one corroborated many times before the school years were over.

In one of his early clinical rotations, Roger was assigned to obstetrics and gynecology. Nerve-racking for any new student, these first few days in the clinic were especially disorienting for someone who could no longer rely on memory to get him through. As a joke on Day One, the residents asked Roger to go to Room 2 and prep the patient for her routine pelvic exam. When he entered the room, he encountered a 400-pound topless go-go dancer named Candy. Already familiar with the approach and in a hurry to get back to her time slot at the pole, Candy had already plopped herself onto the table and assumed the usual position in the stirrups. Anxious to show initiative but confused as to what exactly was expected of him (and devoid of logic), Roger fastened the miner's lamp to his forehead, nestled cautiously onto the squeaky-wheeled three-legged stool, and prepared to get a "head" start on the exam by inserting the prewarmed speculum.

These, of course, were not his instructions (typically, a nurse would be in attendance); it was simply his routine to act before thinking. Shaking uncontrollably during this, his first such exam on a real patient, he fumbled the speculum, which fell to the floor with a jarring clang. As he leaned forward to retrieve it, he inadvertently touched the hot lamp to the inside of the patient's upper thigh. With lightning reflexes, Candy snapped shut her ponderous legs around Roger's head, drawing the miner's lamp even closer to her skin, and bellowed, "Help, help! My meat's on fire!" Candy began to writhe violently from side to side, jerking Roger in a headlock in each direction like a rag doll. Unable to escape the searing sensation, she careened off the table with a thunderous crash, strewing equipment across the floor and taking Roger with her. The din brought racing into the room a crowd of residents who, fortunately, were able to pry apart the giant limbs and extricate Roger from the patient's vise before he was totally asphyxiated. Some time elapsed before Roger would fully regain consciousness and even longer before he would regain composure. His explanation of the details of the event and the wisdom behind his decisions may never have been completely digested by the faculty. Their star student, who only one year before had been admired for his ability to recite the Encyclopedia Britannica from memory, could not muster an iota of common sense.

SLIPPERY WHEN WET

PERHAPS BECAUSE IT COVERS generally happy occasions, the OB-GYN rotation seems to provide a common theater for amusing stories. Students tend to enjoy these weeks in which they are permitted to help in a substantial way with delivering babies. A colleague told me of a third-year student's first clinical mishap in which a slippery newborn infant slid out of his hands. All in the room were aghast but relieved when he drop-kicked the baby back into his own arms. Unlike the student, the baby fortunately suffered no ill effects.

"I guess you've invented a new technique for delivery," quipped the resident.

A lack of common sense is not unique to only young medical students. One colleague remembers walking by the viewing room while two fathers ogled the same newborn baby, each certain that the beautiful baby was his, a scenario that spiraled downward until a fistfight broke out in the middle of the newborn viewing room. It was not as though asking a nurse might have been helpful in settling this question.

There are many more subtle examples of challenges to common sense, even when displayed by some of the most renowned scientists of our times. As a young assistant professor in 1977, I sat in a small conference room with three other junior faculty in a rare informal discussion with the famous Dr. Bernard Lown. The great doctor, one of the lions of cardiology at Harvard, had authored many textbooks and thousands of research papers, and had several syndromes named after him.

Near the end of the Nixon era, when China was opening its doors to the United States, Dr. Lown was invited to join the president's delegation visiting the mainland and to tour the country as the guest of the Chinese minister of health. Lown recounted how he was brought from hospital to hospital to witness patients undergoing major surgery without the support of general anesthesia, the operations apparently performed with just the anesthetic provided by acupuncture. Even patients undergoing lung surgery were wide awake and reading *Chairman Mao's Little Red Book*. At that time, Western medicine's exposure to acupuncture was quite limited, and the lack of double-blind, placebo-controlled trials made Lown understandably skeptical.

So foreign to his way of thinking, the concept of acupuncture as an effective anesthesia prompted Lown to constantly voice his disbelief, suspiciously inquiring of his hosts if they weren't using additional anesthetic. After days of hearing Lown proclaim his constant doubt, the frustrated minister of health grabbed the doctor by the arm and marched him out into a field. There, a donkey was grazing serenely. The Chinese doctor inserted some acupuncture needles into the donkey, took out a scalpel, and sliced open the donkey's abdomen. He then grabbed Lown's arm, shoved it up to the elbow into the abdominal cavity, and walked away. Stunned and left alone in that position for a few minutes, Lown collected his thoughts while the donkey continued to graze, seemingly undisturbed.

Even brilliant scientists memorize and institutionalize a way of doing things, blind to the value of other approaches despite multiple observations. Examples abrade us all the time; we see what we are used to and what we have been familiar with all our lives. Common sense can help teach us to observe anew and open ourselves to change.

It's Just Water from under the Bridge

THE LAPSES IN COMMON SENSE become even thornier as we move from individual to hospital to government. To expand on examples from my experience in Tanzania: As the obvious solutions to certain problems remained unrecognized by those who had grown too accustomed to them to see their way around them, it also became apparent that the only ideas seriously considered had to come from atop the political pecking order. No other solution would be proposed or entertained.

I've mentioned that the hospital's entire water supply system was contaminated with Klebsiella bacteria. In fact, the hospital reportedly had discovered a new strain of Klebsiella by culturing the paint from the walls of the ICU. Nothing had been done about the problem, since replumbing the hospital would require $20 million they did not have.

Initially, I had some difficulty in understanding why there was such a gap in funding this clearly vital project. I had been told that Tanzania's constitution mandated that the government dedicate 15 percent of their GDP to pay for the country's healthcare. I later learned, however, that roughly half of that 15 percent was used to provide free healthcare for government officials and their families anywhere in the world they choose to go. The remaining 7 percent was to come from taxes—but since historically only 40 percent of taxes were collected, only 2.8 percent of GDP remained available for deployment.

As a result, nothing had been done about the contaminated plumbing issue and the widespread infection it spawned. Nearly 90 percent of babies in the unit would become infected with that illness, then transmit it to the mothers who were asked to help the sadly understaffed nurses, and they in turn would bring the infection back to the rest of their families. But it became evident to me that replacement of the entire plumbing network might not even be necessary—that simply irradiating a reservoir of water collected from the main faucets with UV light would confer most of the antiseptic properties needed, and at a fraction of the cost. Because this solution did not come from the desk of the chief of the hospital, however, I doubt it was ever implemented.

I've mentioned that much of the used technical equipment donated to Weill Bugando arrived broken or soon fell into disrepair. These devices, not under warranty, were deemed too expensive to fix, since the necessary replacement parts and accompanying engineers would have to come from far-flung countries. The equipment had been permanently warehoused and remained unused. I asked the hospital to provide me with a detailed inventory of the equipment, a list of the parts that required replacement, their cost, how long they had been broken, and how vital the appliances were to the essential functions of the hospital. Take, for example, the broken ultrasound machine, leaving only one in working order. While replacing the damaged part would not be cheap, the inability to schedule and perform hundreds of necessary ultrasounds both hampered the quality of care and decreased the potential revenue so vital to the hospital's operating budget.

I pointed out that there was no need to get help from Sweden, Switzerland, Germany, Japan, and the United States for individual parts and services; the World Health Organization, which maintains a stockpile of parts, could fill our laundry list at minimal cost compared with purchasing each part from its original manufacturer. Instead, I recommended that they hire a master biomedical technician to come to Tanzania to teach the hospital's repairmen how to bring this equipment back to working order. Mind you, these solutions were hardly mine alone. But the apparent lack of common sense in this environment carries us back to the chapter describing group think and the myopia that permeates the mist of habitual behavior.

MEDI(DOESN'T)CARE

WE HARBOR A FALSE PREMISE that more heads should be expected to see beyond a particular folly, but the opposite is all too often true. Take the regulations Medicare officials imposed that defy common sense. Attempting to contain cost, they blocked cardiologists from performing more than one diagnostic test per patient per office visit. So someone coming in for an examination who needed an echocardiogram as well as a stress test (studies that examine entirely different aspects of heart disease) had to return for one of those tests on a separate day—this to discourage physicians from "bulk ordering" unnecessary tests. For a population such as mine, however, whose patients often traveled a long distance to be examined, the elderly were usually transported by a younger family member who had to miss a day of work or spend extra funds on travel. Of course, I suspect that Medicare secretly hoped that patients would not return for the next test, thus saving the program money. But as it turns out, the cost to Medicare and to the patient to perform both studies on separate visits is, in fact, far greater, and absenteeism from work and lost productivity are only small components of that expense. Patients sent home to wait for their next test are put at risk for heart attacks, arrhythmias, or strokes because of the delay in diagnosis and treatment. More than one patient returned after sustaining an avoidable heart attack that ultimately cost Medicare far more dearly for treatment of resultant congestive heart failure. And for those who succumbed before they could reschedule, the toll was greater yet.

Just in case we hold out hope for some spark of intelligence from wiser, more broad-based organizations that occasionally are asked for a solution to simple equations, here is a sad example that boggles the mind: During the early months of the COVID-19 viral pandemic, large numbers of unfortunate people throughout the country were starved for food, and food banks were woefully depleted. Whether out of fear, hoarding of food that emptied grocery shelves, widespread economic disaster, or supply chain interruption, many counted their pennies to purchase food while gingerly juggling their remaining funds for rent or medication. This balancing act played out in the States and even more throughout the world. But because of a diminished demand for food by so many restaurants throughout the land, farmers and ranchers found themselves sitting on a huge surplus with no immediate place to store it. As a first-pass solution, rather than solve both problems by sending fresh meat, fish, produce, and dairy products to food banks around the country, ranchers and farmers opted to destroy crops and food. In Wisconsin and Ohio, 3.7 million gallons a day of fresh milk were dumped into lagoons and manure pits, millions of pounds of onions were buried in ditches in Idaho, and South Florida farmers plowed beans and cabbage crops back into the soil. Vegetables and fruits were destroyed while more than 750,000 eggs per week were smashed.

Some farmers did subsequently send produce to some food banks, but the wider international distribution of these goods had been deemed "unprofitable" because of fluctuations in currency rates. Weighing the strength of the American dollar against the value of a family or a human life underscores the inanity of this decision. By applying a coordinated algorithm, central government oversight might have turned these tragic practices into ones that could have become examples of common sense and symbols of common decency.

Apparently, the lessons of deductive reasoning so vital to the education of a medical student have not always been absorbed by hospitals or governments.

CHAPTER 19

COMPASSION VS. EMPATHY

OCCASIONALLY MISTAKEN as interchangeable, the words *compassion* and *empathy* hail from different origins. Compassion derives from the Latin roots *com* and *pati*, which means to suffer with, while empathy has its root in the Greek *em* and *pathos*, meaning "in feeling." Superficially these terms seem very much alike, and yet the concept of compassion is more related to one's slightly more distanced, perhaps clinical, appreciation of someone else's pain, but with the additional hope of mitigating the discomfort. Empathy refers to a deep, personal understanding of another's distress. The natural aroma that entices many young students to the field of medicine is one of compassion—the desire to heal as well as to understand.

A bedrock triad of attributes expected of young physicians, known as the three A's—affabilty, availability, and ability—is considered necessary for a compassionate endeavor. Patients expect their doctors to be able, have a right to require that their doctors (or their surrogates) are available, and certainly hope for and deserve ones who are affable. Personifying the three A's, the revered old-world family doctor once gave unlimited access to questions, sacrificed personal family time, and ideally was ever the fountain of compassion.

HEY, DOC, CAN YOU TAKE A LOOK AT THIS?

RECALLING THE MENTORING I RECEIVED from our own family generalist (the one who later attended my medical school graduation) and his true embodiment of the three A's, I renewed the pledge I made to myself in the sixth grade to try to emulate his modeling. During the first few years, I could not of course be expected to properly fulfill the "ability," so I had to rely entirely on "affability" and "availabity" in my dealings with the public.

When I was still a freshman medical student and my parents' friends casually popped over to yodel a neighborly hello and to ask my opinion about their x-rays or EKGs, my knowledge necessarily limited me to only two A's. As time went on, however, these questions became more directed, insistent, convoluted, and important. I remember one evening during services for Yom Kippur—the Jewish Day of Atonement and the most solemn and reflective time of the year—when having fasted for nearly twenty-four hours and standing in prayer I heard a *psst* from the aisle and glimpsed a patient of mine gesturing at me insistently. Fearing some congregant had fainted from dehydration or perhaps collapsed from a heart attack, I shuffled clumsily down the row of seats, stepping on toes and hurrying to a possible emergency in progress.

When I reached my patient, he leaned forward and whispered in my ear: "Doc, do you think my recent cholesterol of 220 is anything to worry about?"

Free advice is a gift not doled out by too many professions. Lawyers and consultants are in the habit of being paid by the fraction of an hour. Stockbrokers despise being chatted up at parties to offer predictions about market trends and recommendations on stock trades, and travel agents do not relish discussions during their evenings out about their preferences for hotels, restaurants, or cruise lines. Respect for time and privacy, not to mention payment for informed expertise, is honored by most. But when friends can no longer contain themselves and overstep their good manners, they are gently reminded.

Compliance with public restraint is not as strict when people are curious, if not desperate, to better understand their medical conditions. Doctors often use terminology that is opaque, offer their thoughts in clipped, rapid-fire speech, work within time-sensitive windows, and impart their conclusions to patients who must try to incorporate the details in an environment of tension.

I have always tried to handle with some grace the many dinner parties at which cholesterol management, hypertension, or drug regimen absorbed the evening's entire conversation, along with sly asides and disparagements regarding the care received at the hands of other doctors. Sometimes the criticisms leveled at colleagues were either untrue or unfair, sometimes true but misquoted, and typically misunderstood. Absent a complete set of circumstances, I was usually left with only the tools of a knowing nod. One evening at the start of a black-tie charity ball, I was pinned into a corner near the "Dining Out" section of the silent auction by a parade of current and former patients who had stockpiled their medical queries. The line formed to the right, and the cavalcade lasted more than an hour. Having not eaten since early morning, I was starving and light-headed. And for the first time in my recent memory, I began to pray for the program to begin.

As I managed to extricate myself enough to slalom my way toward the dinner table, I was blindsided by an elderly woman in a long black gown with sequined spaghetti straps. She beckoned me to follow her around a screen that hid a pile of unserved entrées. I followed her quickly, fearing she was in real distress or possibly at risk.

She spun around to confront me and asked, "Would you mind just taking a quick peek at the scar of my pacemaker site?"

I asked, "Does it hurt, do you think it might be infected, or is there something about it that is bothering you?"

"Oh no," she replied. "You put the pacemaker in about four years ago, and it hasn't bothered me a bit. It seems fine. I just thought it was about time to take another look at it."

"Of course," I responded to her with a wink. "Undress, please."

From the French Revolution:
The Tongue Is the Enemy of the Neck

DURING ALL MY YEARS OF PRACTICE, I found it easiest to be on call for my own patients every night, rather than split the week with partners and have several evenings free. Since I knew their medical conditions best, I felt I could respond more directly and make better decisions on their behalf. That knowledge gave me the power to choose with some sense of certainty and calm whether, if called, I could roll over and go back to sleep, or if I needed to race off to the emergency room at 2:00 a.m.

For most of my colleagues who trained and practiced under similar conditions, it would be understandable if being interrupted during the occasional social outing with a barrage of medical questions provoked mild resentment. Yet despite this common intrusion, I have found physicians to be open about answering politely and informatively. There are, of course, medicolegal risks inherent in providing advice without proper information.

The well-known case so widely reported from Boston described a fellow trimming the hedges on his front lawn one Sunday morning. He had lived next to his friend, a neurologist, for the past fifteen years. This brisk morning, they were both clipping the same bush from opposite sides when the conversation began.

"Hey, John," the neighbor said to the neurologist. "You know, I've had a little headache on and off for the past couple of days. What do you think I ought to do?"

"Well, that depends on how much it hurts, if it's always in the same spot, and if you have any other symptoms along with it, like numbness, weakness, visual trouble. That kind of thing," replied the doctor.

"To be honest, it is pretty mild—mostly in the back of my head. I really don't notice anything else."

"Okay, I would just see if it goes away in a day or so, but if it persists, why don't you just drop by the office and let me take a closer look."

Since the neurologist never heard back from his neighbor, he assumed his friend's problem had resolved. As one might fear, however, the sad fellow ignored the neurologist's advice and was later diagnosed with brain cancer that had rapidly metastasized during the ensuing weeks. He'd never dropped by the office, nor had he even knocked on his neighbor's door. After the tumor was discovered, the man sued the neurologist because, in the eyes of the law, the front-lawn chat represented a professional consultation. The court judged that the neurologist failed in his obligation to call his friend back in a few days when he had not heard from him, just to be sure he was following doctor's orders. The neurologist was found liable and lost the suit.

Casual sidewalk medical banter sometimes comes with a price. Even if during a "harmless" social exchange, a doctor gingerly questions the validity of a therapeutic decision made by another colleague, he may find himself exposed to legal action. More than one legal battle was born after a doctor-friend was pressed into commenting on a therapy during a cocktail party. Offering a formal departure from a colleague's opinion may incite personal animosity as well as legal retribution and may impede the dissemination of real and potentially valuable alternatives. On several occasions I have been asked to defend colleagues who, after providing a second opinion, were being sued by one notorious, litigious cardiologist whose medical decisions they challenged. In one case, I found myself personally on the defense as well.

Sometime in 1980, in the early days of my medical practice, I attended a dinner party at which I was introduced to a young woman whose mother had just undergone a balloon angioplasty. Three months had passed since her procedure, and her mother once again began to suffer from chest pain. The young woman complained that the doctor had been obtrusive in his response to her concerns, and she was simply asking me if these symptoms were typical after a balloon procedure. These were the years before sophisticated balloon technology or coated stents had been developed, so I understood that there was a very real danger that the woman's coronary artery was becoming blocked once again. Furthermore, the timing between the balloon procedure and resumption of pain of just a few months suggested a serious risk.

Six days later, the patient came to my office to tell me she had demanded further attention to her symptoms from her cardiologist. He performed a repeat catheterization, confirming the near closure of her left main coronary artery near the site of her ballooning, but with scar tissue extending into a treacherous location. Even with today's technology, a balloon and stent of the left main coronary is fraught with major risk.

Having seen the follow-up results, it was my opinion (and conventional wisdom) that she should undergo bypass surgery. She proceeded with my recommendation and was discharged from the hospital without complication after a week. Two weeks thereafter, I received two documents in the mail: the first, a copy of an inflammatory letter her doctor sent her indicating she had interrupted vital research with which he was involved; the second, a letter from his attorney threatening to sue me for slander.

As it turned out, this ploy of extortion had been played out several times in our community by this physician, leaving three other colleagues of mine in a puddle. I was contacted by the chairman of the department of medicine at our hospital to ask if I would be willing to testify against the doctor if the hospital promised to indemnify me. The cardiologist arrived at the hearings flanked by two attorneys, but following a highly charged give-and-take during a three-hour exchange of facts and cross-examination, his privileges at the hospital were revoked and the suits against me and the other three physicians were dropped. Such can be the outcome of the "casual discussion" of medicine at social gatherings.

Lox and Vagals

Somehow, despite the ambience of medicolegal activity that threatens to dissuade physicians from responding to the public's occasional spontaneous cries for help, there will always be those who step forward to be of service, as evidenced by the following encounter relayed by an endocrinologist colleague of mine.

While at a conference in Miami, my friend was lunching at a kosher deli near his hotel. The mostly Jewish clientele was elderly, so it was of some concern when the frantic plea sounded, "Is there a doctor in the house?"

Responding to the alarm, my friend was led into the ladies' room to find a pale octogenarian sitting on the tile floor, clutching her chest. From all descriptions, she was the quintessential Jewish grandmother with the classic Polish-New York accent.

"How can I help you?" asked the doctor. "How are you not feeling well?"

"Vell, I am having a little chest pain and some trouble breathing, but I'll be fine in a minute," she whimpered with interrupted respirations and beads of perspiration coalescing on her forehead.

After taking a brief history that reflected a full house of cardiac risk factors, the doctor recommended he call an ambulance to transport her to the local hospital.

"Oy vey no," she objected. "I'm going to be okay. I don't vant to go to a hospital. Really!"

The next several minutes of debate—advice-turned-to-persuasion vs. defense—arrived at a standoff. Slumping down to sit on the bathroom floor next to the woman, the doctor refused to give up.

"Mrs. Goldstein, your symptoms are serious and need to be attended to by a doctor."

She finally acquiesced with, "Okay, okay! I vill go to see my dactah… tomorrow."

"And where does your doctor live?" he inquired suspiciously.

"By New York," she said.

Bringing his face close to hers to make this point crystal clear, the doctor emphasized, "Mrs. Goldstein, you cannot fly on an airplane. You are having a serious problem, and you must see a doctor now! If you delay much longer, you could die."

With a sweet glint in her eye and the kind of demure smile that has persuaded Jewish men to do such women's bidding for centuries, Mrs.

Goldstein leaned in, softly pinched the doctor's cheek, and asked, "Vill *you* be my dactah?"

His years of practicing the charm offensive paid off. He embodied the three A's.

I'VE GOT YOUR NUMBER, DOCTOR

TO MAKE GOOD ON THEIR PLEDGE to be available (affable and able already an assumption), concierge physicians began a movement to respond to the increasing demand for personalized healthcare. With the aging of America, a greater proportion of the population will be enrolling in Medicare programs—a system for which there is significant additional pressure to expand coverage and services across a wider public domain. As I have hinted, one great concern is that possession of a Medicare card will not be synonymous with doctor access.

Multitiered systems of medical practice have been around for a long time, among the most celebrated being the one developed in the United Kingdom. Harley Street, world famous for its concentration of private physicians, was founded by 20 practitioners in 1860 and expanded to about 200 in 1914 and 1,500 or so by 1948, when the National Health Service was launched. Today there are more than 5,000 physicians working in the area, with an escalating pressure to circumvent a system well known to suffer from long wait times. Public health experts predict a further increase of 40 percent in private hospital capacity in the UK from 2018 to 2023.

Celebrated names in American medicine have always attracted an elite list of patients to their offices. A few years before Medicare was introduced to the United States, a select group of physicians with worldwide reputations chose to limit their practices to small numbers of patients to provide exceptional care and to afford the time needed to investigate thorny therapies. Dr. Myron Prinzmetal, a renowned cardiologist in Los Angeles in the 1960s, began to craft a practice that some would say was the forerunner of the concierge movement. But the first recognizable wave of concierge medicine began in 1990 in Seattle, expanding to more than 12,000 practices in the US by 2014.

The concierge doctor functions by paring her patient roster from several thousand to perhaps 400–600 active charts. Doing so assures her clientele constant contact, easy access, hospital advocacy, fast response times, and her personalized interpretation of diagnostic data and therapeutic options. Additionally, she benefits by being able to maneuver in a less stressful, less cluttered environment, improving her success in fulfilling the affable and able moieties of the three A's formula. Marrying the desire to spend quality time with her patients while mitigating her rising office overhead costs (plus accelerating repayment of medical-school debt), the concierge doctor accomplishes her goal by exacting an annual retainer. Membership fees vary widely depending on specialty, location, and what the market will bear. Some family practice offices charge a few hundred dollars a year, while fees for distinguished practitioners can soar to upward of $40,000 per year.

The justification for some fees is understandable. Medicine may be the only profession in which time spent on behalf of, but not face-to-face with, a client offers no compensation. Certainly, lawyers and other consultants charge hourly rates in recognition of the time spent for services rendered, including travel time. Doctors have not previously charged for answering midnight calls, responding to questions from the emergency room, consulting by telephone with other doctors, refilling prescriptions, interpreting blood tests, or debating with insurance companies over the medical necessity of ordering certain tests. In fact, when I was once asked to provide a second opinion for a patient being considered for a possible heart-lung transplant and spent hours reviewing a panoply of scans performed in Florida, I did so free of charge. And had I even wanted remuneration for the eight hours on the Sunday I spent examining the tests, I would have found no way to do it, since there were no billing codes to apply for such a charge, or for any of the "free" services just listed.

For the GP, pediatrician, and even the internist, whose incomes are primarily dependent on direct patient contact rather than testing, the time spent on uncompensated activities can crush a practice. Increasing costs from computer services, office rental, malpractice insurance, lack of recourse in dealing with mounting patients' accounts receivable, employee salaries, and lowered insurance reimbursement can pressure a physician to offset overhead by instituting a fee structure.

The concierge model affords doctors the chance to continue to provide excellent medical care for the few, but dislocates the many at a time when the doctor shortage, or at least its maldistribution, deepens across the country. Loyal patients who may have been enrolled in the same doctor's office for many years but who cannot afford the new annual concierge fee are thus dislodged and compelled to seek another provider. Often these are elderly patients who may have difficulty finding a practitioner who is willing to take on new Medicare patients, since reimbursement is often so meager. My own parents were "fired" by their internist in Florida after being part of his practice for fifteen years because, he admitted, ministering to their healthcare needs had become too time-consuming. As the high-profile doctor to my father, the rabbi, he had enjoyed the benefits of a huge referral from my father's congregants; now that he had to earn his stellar reputation, the effort required to be a real caregiver seemed excessive.

Concierge practices construct an arrangement by which participating patients jump to the head of the line and lock the door behind them. The latecomers and the elderly—often those with the greatest need—are sometimes given little notice and left to fend for themselves, having to scour the neighborhood for a competent practitioner. From the perspective of the disenfranchised, how can we deny the impression that this model risks constructing a formula that diminishes compassion by the doctor for all patients and blunts empathy for others by the concierge enrollee?

CHAPTER 20

THE BAD NEWS BEARERS

I CANNOT REALLY KNOW how much thought other premed students might have given to a time when they would have to deliver bad news to a patient. As for me, I was at first so bloated with the image of becoming the white knight striding into a waiting room to offer a frightened family the gift of my triumphant cure that I rarely considered the alternative. But since disease eventually wins, the delivery of tragic news is unavoidable. Except for the clergy, I can think of few other groups of grad students who find themselves in this disturbing position, nor can I think of any way a student can emotionally prepare for it.

Of course, we all understood there would inevitably be days when we would suffer unfair loss, witness even sound judgments gone awry, and sustain a wrenching, bitter, gnawing pain. There would also be nights of intense self-doubt, deep remorse, self-criticism, and erosive disturbances of the soul. In time I worried: Would the words I offered, the sentiments I displayed be apropos? Would they confer solace, inspire acceptance, unburden guilt, provide understanding, engender faith? Would they be barely adequate or more than enough, a nightmare or an uplifting dream, a perpetual wound or an enduring gift?

But these worries would be held in abeyance for a few years. As a mere medical student, I was grateful for my resident or attending to bear the brunt of the sad interaction with patient or family. I was, however, always keen to observe, absorb, and amass words and phrases I found genuine and effective. Looking into the face of a patient, inspecting the body language of a family, I came to appreciate what was done well and what was not. After the verdict was imparted, I could see whose eyes were vacant, tearful, or hopeful; whose shoulders were stiff, heaving, or broken; who was enlightened or befuddled or in shock. Still, these were solely intellectual exercises that, while practical, gave me no inkling as to how it truly felt to be the deliverer. I was not yet challenged to face my own patients, not yet held responsible for their outcomes.

It soon became clear to me that confronting a family unprepared for the worst was an uneasy task for some attending physicians. In fact, the experience was so unpleasant that during my third year of school, some attendings would send me in to administer the first frontal blow and absorb the counterpunch. Their feeble excuses typically alluded to busy schedules, their need to race off to visit another patient in extremis, or their wish to teach me an important lesson. I saw this fraud as a sign of their cowardice but accepted it as an uncomfortable opportunity to grow and play a pivotal role in the final journey of a patient's life.

FIRST THEORY, THEN A REALITY CHECK

AS A JUNIOR, my first such solo encounter involved a lithe eighteen-year-old girl who was hospitalized with mild abdominal pain. Charmingly freckled and sporting an impressive six-pack, she had been an athlete during her freshman year of college, juggling a rigorous jazz dance schedule with her varsity field hockey scholarship. Even the tight ringlets in her reddish-brown hair exuded a muscular energy. Despite her discomfort and perhaps a sense of foreboding, she maintained the matter-of-fact demeanor of a competitor, preferring to attribute her recent weight loss to a dedicated exercise ethic.

In contrast to today, medical insurance in the late 1960s offered doctors the chance to admit patients to the hospital for diagnostic testing, so when we first met, my innocent freshman did not yet appear to be acutely ill. Tutored in the powerful secrets of the physical exam, also a sign of the times, I carefully palpated, percussed, and listened. The prominence of a subtle but significant left-sided mass on abdominal examination was the clue that led me to uncover the target of its treachery. The patient was found to have an advanced angiosarcoma, a rare and malignant cancer of the blood vessels of the spleen with extensive metastasis to the liver. Her future was dark, the prognosis dismal. My attending felt no compunction to assign me the duty to convey to her the diagnosis and its implications.

In a puddle of sweat and with great trepidation, I leaked slowly into her room like water seeping under the door. It seemed like minutes had passed before all of me had fully entered. As I hesitantly approached the bedside, I found her staring out the window, insulated, sheltered, and swaddled by her thoughts. I pierced that bubble with some inane small talk, hoping to put both of us at ease, but I soon realized that I had substituted college party banter for appropriate bedside manner. Clearly, she was focused on the reason for my visit, searching my face with a scrutiny that burned my skin.

I initially sought some neutral ground by describing the cell morphology and biochemical characteristics of her tumor. I talked a lot about her blood work and test results, putting up med-speak buffers whenever her eyes darkened or lips pouted, suggesting she might have perceived the tragic ramifications of my soliloquy. And finally, there was a long... clumsy... uneasy... graceless... mortified pause. I had depleted my store of medical trivia with which to baffle her and needed to bring our discussion to its heartbreaking conclusion. My pulse was galloping, frantically searching for an escape from my chest and the room. Beads of sweat coalesced on my forehead, my breathing quickened, I began to feel lightheaded, and then could not hold back a small plague of tears.

Could I have been more awkward, less professional, or more aware of my own emotions rather than hers? I sincerely doubt it. I gave her nothing she wanted and nothing she needed. Despite hearing her death sentence for the first time, she acted as if I were the sicker of the two of us, and with poise and compassion she intuited the pain that I was going through. Her merciful smile partially revived me. I composed myself and sheepishly crawled back out of my self-absorbed abyss. I did not sob again... at least not out loud, until I attended her funeral two weeks later.

The recollection of this first traumatic event smoldered as I burdened new patients and families with the anvil of doom, that experience having been a primer for future anguish. Yet even as I got better at delivering bad news with greater calm and professionalism, I never knew when I'd once again suddenly feel undone and blindsided. Ten years or so later, I was catapulted right back to that caustic memory. A twenty-four-year-old man presented to an outlying emergency room complaining of chest pain. His initial EKG was apparently normal, even though his symptoms were typical for angina. Given his age and absent cardiac risk factors, his doctors wasted precious time in disbelief, pondering options and passively observing his evolving heart attack, then transferred him to our ER only after the laboratory data was painfully obvious.

By the time I came to the bedside, the young man was in cardiogenic shock, so I moved him emergently to the catheterization laboratory for both diagnostic and therapeutic purposes. A large clot obstructed his proximal left anterior descending coronary artery. These were the days before stents had been invented, and every balloon I used to prop open the artery failed. The dilation attempt was like sticking my finger into a vat of chocolate pudding; upon withdrawal, the contents immediately re-obliterated the vessel. Despite my directly infusing massive anticoagulants and supporting his vital signs, the patient tragically succumbed.

The rest of the experience for me was like ripping a bandage off a fresh, bloody wound. My wretched task was to walk back to the waiting room to inform a frightened young woman that her fiancé had died. To this day I can still reconstruct the deafening absence of sound made by her open mouth and paralyzed vocal cords. Her eyes pleaded with mine, searching for a retraction, desperate to be awakened from a nightmare, begging for literal change of heart.

When I asked colleagues if they could recollect their first similar experience after fifty years of practice, each had cloistered the details of those encounters into their memory crypt with indelible sadness. One obstetrician remembers his horror and disorientation as a first-year medical student while tagging along with his uncle, a pathologist, on weekends performing autopsies on babies and teens with cystic fibrosis. As a naive voyeur, however, he had no direct contact with these tragic figures before they died, so his torment was less intimate, less personal. In his third year of school, however, he took an elective in hematology and was assigned the care of a woman in her twenties who was being treated for leukemia. The morning after his patient had failed a bone marrow transplant procedure, he arrived at the hospital and was approached by his resident.

"Have you ever taken care of a patient who died?" asked the resident.

"No," replied the student, apprehension now creeping into his voice.

"Then why don't you just peek into that hospital room over there?" the resident suggested, orienting him toward the door occupied by his patient with leukemia.

To this day, the obstetrician remembers the name and specific lab data identifying this, his first head-on collision with death.

Another physician talks about being sent into a room to work up a young man who was about his own age. The moment his new patient disrobed, the student took one look at his abdomen and knew he was terminal. In the ensuing six weeks of surgery, chemotherapy, long hours monitoring fragile vital signs, and late-night philosophical discussions about death and the hereafter, the battle was finally lost. For the student who shared a relationship, the emotional contract was suddenly ruptured, and a change was now expected. His patient-confidant had now become a practical learning tool, and those opportunities were rarely squandered. Two hours after his patient died, the student was required to participate in his autopsy. For the second time in his young medical training, he lost his lunch.

Yet another physician remembers his early introduction to examining young patients with leukemia. He could intuit even in those earlier days that some would survive and some would not. Determined to remain strong and to avoid emotional entanglement that could undermine his efficacy, he pledged to himself to stay aloof and clinical, refusing to allow any gap in the chain mail that could expose his defenses. A few days after this internal edict, he and his classmates met with Dr. Carl Moore, the chief of hematology and former chief of medicine at Washington University. The students were going through a training exercise in which they drew their own blood sample, made a slide, and examined it under the microscope. One of the students had difficulty identifying his own blood cells and called Dr. Moore to give him a hand. That was the day the student learned he had leukemia. It was also the day my colleague came to know just how vulnerable he really was.

CLINICAL EXPERIENCE: THE GREAT AND CRUEL TEACHER

MOST OF US HAVE NO DIFFICULTY mourning those close to us, those whom we knew and loved. With a heavy heart we endure the bittersweet experience of traveling with a family member or a friend through their final passage. And we can hear or read about people even removed from our immediate circle of influence who have died, and can feel sorrow and sympathy for their loss. Moreover, we, of course, are outraged when we hear about mass shootings, or crestfallen when we view coverage of the COVID-19 death toll.

Yet from the perspective of a young student, the loss of a patient whose life has intersected with hers, however briefly, even tangentially, carries with it a unique combination of grief, guilt, and an impotence that is difficult to describe. This, too, is vital to the transition a student must make on the way to becoming a doctor, a wound reserved for clergy and workers in the field of medicine. Over the span of a physician's lifetime, engaging in mortal combat with disease has the potential to replay itself often enough to deposit layer upon layer of history, like growth rings within a tree. With time, the tree gains strength, resilience, ... and occasionally rigidity.

I knew there would be many more lacerations over the course of my career, and I prayed that I would do a better job as I gained experience and maturity. Even more, I hoped that I would learn to handle upheaval more easily, develop an emotional callus without becoming callous, find a way to console without carrying the burden home with me. I wanted each future encounter to hurt but not destroy, to cut but not scar. In my naivete, I did not yet understand how impossible it would be to achieve that kind of balance. Every patient was different, each defeat a personal condemnation bearing the weight of "if only." For me, ushering in death was never to be characterized by the golden mean.

Even as a student, I recognized it would always be a struggle. With time, I learned to suppress my thoughts during the day, throughout dinner with the family, while reading the children a bedtime story. For my own protection, I was compelled to compartmentalize my heartache. But late at night the questions would swirl; the alternatives would be rehashed, warmed over; and the enzymes of anguish would digest my spirit. Self-forgiveness is a gift we somehow must either inherit or cultivate in a garden we tend. We eventually learn to bury yesterday in a file marked Clinical Experience and direct the next day's attention to the fresh wars we are forced to wage. This focus becomes a vital mechanism of self-preservation.

CHAPTER 21

FAITH AND MEDICINE:
IS THE DOCTOR
THE ONLY GOD IN THE HOUSE?

SIR WILLIAM OSLER, the 19th-century physician universally recognized as the father of modern medicine, once said, "Without faith a man can do nothing; with it all things are possible." Dr. Osler left McGill University in 1884 and later joined the new Johns Hopkins School of Medicine in 1889. When I was an undergraduate at McGill and came across this quote, it always puzzled me. Osler implies but does not specify the source of this inspiration of faith: Is he referring to faith in self, science, medicine, or God? We might also ask if the individual he encourages to have faith is the doctor or the patient.

The proposition that patients must have faith in their doctor is well established, but one may easily point out that patients need not believe in their doctor or the antibiotic prescribed to resolve their pneumonia for that medication to work. Patients arriving at an emergency room in a coma have no access to a conscious silo of faith, hope, or despair that might affect their response to therapy. Obviously, it is not an imperative to have trust in one's doctor for an appropriate therapy to be effective.

There are, however, many studies that examine the subtle impact that trust in a patient's medical team plays. The most straightforward variable is compliance. A patient who believes in a doctor's decisions will often choose to continue taking the prescribed medication. Those patients who subscribe to conspiracy theories, fall victim to snake-oil scam artists, or abandon all scientifically proven treatment are more likely to impede improvement.

ADVICE AND CONSENT: THE VALUE OF DOUBLE-BLIND FAITH

ABANDONING VACCINATION PROGRAMS out of fear that vaccines contain ingredients promoting autism exemplifies one of the most recent examples of loss of trust. The CDC has conducted nine trials since 2003 that failed to demonstrate a link to autism following measles, mumps, or rubella vaccine. Thimerosal, a mercury-based ingredient used as a preservative to mitigate contamination of multidose batches, has been shown to exert no effect on the incidence of autism but nonetheless has been removed from most vaccine formulas. As expected, the impact of this lack of faith has resulted in significant illness. The World Health Organization estimates 2 to 3 million deaths each year are prevented by immunization for diphtheria, tetanus, whooping cough, and measles. In the United States, the most common deaths preventable by vaccines are influenza, hepatitis, and tuberculosis.

We have been asked to overcome political and religious bias most emphatically in our preventative and therapeutic choices for COVID-19. As worldwide experience with this pandemic has evolved and shaped both our knowledge of the science and the recommendations made by the CDC, NIH, and FDA, it seems understandable that skepticism might erode our faith in these institutions. It is easy to forget how quickly the data accumulated and how this impacted the process of medicine, which then necessarily called for modifications to earlier public precautions. Uncharacteristic of medical journalism, the race to publish seemed to overwhelm the usual caution applied by editorial staffs of even the most august and respected journals—the result being the unprecedented retraction of scientific articles whose methodology was questionable. And the public's faith in medicine continued to dwindle.

The media played into our partisanship on vaccine safety by highlighting the same information from opposite viewpoints. For example: When clots were discovered in patients after receiving the J&J vaccine, one could imagine headlines as diverse as "Blood Clots in Six Patients Linked to J&J Vaccine" and "Far Fewer Clots Identified in Patients Receiving J&J Vaccine than in COVID-19."

Faith in our public health officials need not be blind, but conspiracies that could jeopardize millions of lives should play no role in determining guidelines for vaccination; it comes down to analyzing the potential detrimental impact of preventative intervention vs. exposure to known life-threatening infection.

The more nuanced factor associated with a lack of faith is evident in the designs used in clinical research trials. As evidence-based medicine became central to our understanding of how scientific knowledge progresses, we learned the pitfalls of unblinded studies. Advertisements targeting the lay public are full of testimonials and casual observations that tempt readers or viewers into believing unproven therapies. Subtle bias creeps into research conclusions when controlled studies are abandoned. When a patient knows she is getting the trial drug rather than the placebo, she is more likely to derive benefit if she has faith in her doctor or hope for the experiment. And even if her expectations of benefit waver, her subconscious desire to support her doctor often colors her response. These unblinded results do not always stand up to the scrutiny of future controlled protocols, especially if the study design limits the assertion of benefit to a short time.

Further, if the doctor knows which patient is receiving the experimental agent, his faith in the value of the trial therapy shades the way he interacts with his patient, introducing a subtle positive blush that sullies the integrity of the results. Thus, the double-blind/placebo/control trial —in which patients do not know whether they've received the drug or the control and doctors do not know to which patients they gave the drug or control—has become the preferred methodology to overcome the influence of faith.

Beyond the basic assumption that a successful doctor-patient relationship must ideally be built on faith in each other, two even more stringent levels of confidence require farsighted trust. The first involves the patient's willingness to accept *informed consent*. There is a natural tendency for hopeful patients to hear only the upside potential for a procedure or surgery. The desire to be healthy and the will to live are strong magnets for optimism. Statistics notwithstanding, we are hellbent to place our outcomes within the best slope of the bell-shaped curve. Even pessimists by nature often resist a negative prognosis, shielding themselves from a reality too heavy to consider. The patient trusts the doctor's explanation of relative risk, believing in the doctor's expertise in navigating around the complications that may have beset less-skilled practitioners elsewhere in the world. Informed consent offers patients a contract that obligates them to a course of therapy but demands no assurance of success from the doctor so long as the doctor's actions do not fall below the standard of care in that specialty.

The contract is an entirely different vehicle than that signed between a homeowner and the builder who promises to deliver a product that is found acceptable and to predetermined specifications. Informed consents are frequently signed by patients who haven't read the fine print, and even more often without their knowing the incidence with which complications are known to occur. Especially in new, innovative, and difficult procedures, the consent form usually quotes the success rates published by the physician who developed the intervention and at the institution with the most clinical experience rather than the personal and local statistics of the treating physician. Acknowledging that some doctors are notorious for having an excess of faith in themselves, their assessment of their own success rates may be overestimated. (On more than one occasion, I have asked a surgeon to return my patient to the operating room for symptoms of excessive bleeding. Only once—following a hip replacement—however, did an orthopedist protest that his patients never bleed! He was wrong.) You can see why, given all these innuendos, informed consent really does require faith on the part of the patient.

After acutely rupturing a disc in my neck, I sustained complete paralysis of my right arm several hours before going into emergency surgery. Time was of the essence, as further delay threatened to make the paralysis permanent, so the trivialities of an exhaustive informed consent were bypassed. Awakened the next morning by the nurse at the hospital, I was asked how I felt during the night.

"I slept pretty well, and the horrendous pain is gone," I said. "But my arm is still paralyzed."

Her smiling retort was, "Oh well—you win some, and you lose some!"

Fortunately, I understood enough about neurology to put her casual and irresponsible comment into perspective, realizing my paralysis was likely to be temporary, which was exactly the case when the surgeon quickly alleviated the nerve impingement. Sadly, the advantage I had of knowledge and experience is not available to most; when those patients hear such careless words uttered by a nurse, that gap of information can easily shake their faith in both doctors and their staff.

Deuteronomy: "Therefore Choose Life"

Some would say that the greatest requirement of faith in the doctor takes place during the discussions of living wills, or end-of-life directives. As a student, I occasionally eavesdropped on the crafting of such documents by my attending physician with his patients or with their families. And when I was assigned to care for such a patient during my third or fourth year, I would always go back to the bedside (or to the family waiting room) later in the day to determine if the ramifications of the directive were clearly understood. They almost never were.

The opportunity to clarify end-of-life directives with my patients during my student years prepared me for future assaults I might never have anticipated. Here is an example: For nearly thirty years, I cared for a woman who was born in the Bronx but who moved to Houston later in life to be closer to her family following a bout of worsening COPD and congestive heart failure. She had sustained a large heart attack in 1984 and ever since had been living a sedate, restrictive life with her devoted daughter and successful son-in-law.

She made an appointment to see me in my office with her daughter one afternoon, complaining of chest pain, and as I started to take her history, she began to rapidly decompensate. I quickly notified the ER, called for an emergency elevator, and loaded her on to a gurney to personally escort her over the elevated crosswalk to the hospital. No sooner had the elevator doors closed when the patient arrested, and I initiated CPR. Arriving on the second floor, our proximity to a defibrillator maximized my chances for success. Following her brief stabilization, I moved her to a catheterization room and performed an emergency angioplasty and stent placement, and she survived to be discharged from the hospital a few days thereafter.

When she returned to the office in her wheelchair one week later, she was once again accompanied by her daughter, whose husband lagged behind to corner a private chat with me right outside the exam room door.

"I just don't know how we could possibly thank you enough for saving my mother-in-law's life," he said. "What you did was extraordinary, and I thought I could begin to express our gratitude with this little gift."

He extended a hand that caressed a vintage bottle of Opus One cabernet that he had treasured for the past decade.

"Mom is pretty frail, you know, and I kind of doubt she would be able to survive another attack like this one. So I think maybe we should agree that in case of another arrest, we should not perform CPR," he stammered clumsily, eyes demurely inspecting the carpet. "I think it might be best for everyone," he whispered.

"Oh, I see," I responded, trying to appear matter-of-fact. "Well, have you discussed this with Mom?"

"God, no!" he exclaimed, eyes bulging and still clutching the precious bottle with which he was hoping to seal the deal. "I ... I think this should just be our little secret. I mean, I haven't even told my wife, but I'm quite sure she would agree."

"Well, okay then. Why don't we simply go on in there and ask her right now if that is what she wants?" I said, pushing the hot button.

"No, no, no!! We need to keep this discreet," he insisted. "We don't want to bother her with this, do we? She's already in a wheelchair. I was hoping this would be just between the two of us."

"Oh, well, she's already in a wheelchair," I replied, "so why don't you just push her down the stairs, then?"

And with that, I opened the door to the exam room and bounced in with the enthusiasm of a late-night TV host starting his monologue, the son-in-law doing a credible Eeyore imitation, limping in behind me. By this time I assumed the wine had been taken off the proverbial table.

"Hi, honey pie. I am so glad to see you here!" I smiled at my round-faced patient with hair dyed the same burnt orange as the official school color of the University of Texas. "I have an essential question to discuss with you, now that things have stabilized. We all realize you have been through a lot lately. And you know, this kind of cardiac event could recur unpredictably at any time. So I think it is important that we are all on the same page. Right?" I interrogated the three other pairs of eyes in the room one at a time, each betraying their owner's thoughts.

I measured each word cautiously and with purpose: "If you knew there would come a day when another heart attack would occur, and that another CPR was necessary if you arrested, what do you want me to do? Would you want me to do all I could to save you? Are you tired of it all?"

"Dr. Klein," she responded hesitantly, slathering each word in her thick New York accent. Gazing mournfully at her lap below the rhinestone rim of her bifocals, she picked at her crisp cotton dress and then looked up, eyebrows raised to meet my gaze with pleading intensity. "I want to live!"

I paused a moment and reached over to cup her hand gently in mine. We had the advantage of having built a bond between us over many years. "And so you shall, if I have anything to do with it," I announced with a wink and a grin of reassurance. With that, her daughter's contorted face relaxed and joined me in a smile. Her son-in-law played along, feigning relief at our consensus and pretending disappointment when I respectfully declined to accept his bottle of souring grapes.

Living Wills That Take Dead Aim

THE ETHICS OF LIVING WILLS, which have been the subject of numerous papers and theses, deserve far deeper study than can be provided here. Living wills conceived in a doctor's office when a patient is feeling well often focus on theoretical circumstances under which interventions such as defibrillation (shock), resuscitation, pacemaker implantation, or respirator assistance might be withheld. The vast majority agree that prolonging life without a hope of meaningful existence is unwarranted. But too frequently the directives are succinct and have not considered, for example, an option to intubate as a stabilizing strategy for a potentially reversible illness. Multiple studies published from the US, UK, Israel, and Asia have quantified the survival rates for patients placed on acute ventilatory support. Ignoring, for purposes of discussion, the obviously important variables of age and causes of respiratory failure, the overall mortality rate seems to consistently average 38 percent across all countries. If patients knew that two-thirds of those placed on a ventilator would ultimately be extubated and survive, they might modify the absolute restrictions imposed by the advanced directive they sign.

The same is true for insertion of a temporary or permanent pacemaker. Many people have no idea how relatively atraumatic the implanting of a pacemaker really is and may not fully appreciate the degree to which a permanent pacemaker can purchase for their loved one roughly four to eight more years of life.

Long-term benefits may also accrue from resuscitative efforts, although the length of additional time attained from this procedure is obviously dependent on the disease process, the age of the patient, and even the reporting institution. In-hospital defibrillation, first developed at Johns

Hopkins in 1957, using a 200-pound portable machine, is successful today 90 percent of the time if performed within the first minute after cardiac arrest, with an attrition rate of 7–10 percent for every minute of delay. While families may be dismayed by the knowledge that only 25–48 percent of these initial survivors will live to be discharged from the hospital, the gain is far from insignificant and in many cases presents better odds than hoped for in the treatment of some malignancies. If a daughter learned that, regardless of diagnosis, her father would survive and be discharged from the hospital almost half the time, would she use that information to amend his living will? And what if she was told that when CPR alone is required, the one-year survival exceeds 70 percent, while 28 percent live for another nine years? How would disclosure of those data enlighten a family?

A living will, constructed years in advance but now out of date, can shackle an ER physician from performing what might have been a successful resuscitative effort, one that could have potentially resurrected a long and meaningful life. The need to constantly update these restrictions, as medical circumstances may emergently dictate, becomes impractical and challenging, if not impossible. What alternatives do we have?

The fluidity of healthcare conditions stresses more than ever the need for faith in the doctor. Having observed during my student days how confusing advanced directives could be, I became determined to promise my future patients (and their families) that I would do everything necessary to support their desires to continue to lead a meaningful life. They needed to understand that this approach could mean giving me license to ignore their sweeping directives to avoid intubation or CPR if I held out reasonable hope for their loved one's meaningful recovery. With this stipulation, I was almost always permitted to revise these instructions as I saw fit once I had explained the principles behind my convictions. So long as the family had faith that I would let them know the moment the future darkened and all was lost, our compact was secure.

Thankfully, the doctor-family-patient trust is often shared with others in the acute and chronic final moments. The ER doctor, hospitalist, nurse, and intensive care unit specialist are all empowered to interpret the living will as written. And in a milieu in which the death march processes at a slower pace, the hospice care team dramatically intervenes to cushion the end journey when a DNR (do not resuscitate) order is in place. The compassionate treatment and sensitive interchange from the hospice team has lent the family and the patient reassurance of a consistent strategy during the waning hours. To decipher the wishes of every heart and to offer dignity for every life, plans must be individualized, details meticulous, understanding complete, and the wellsprings of faith deep indeed.

DNR? HEAVEN KNOWS

ANY REASONABLE OVERLAP between faith and medicine must address the positions taken by various religions when it comes to advanced directives, but an in-depth treatment of religious doctrines in relation to the principles of end of life is beyond the reach of this book. Even the most superficial overview will provide little color to the depth with which senior clergy and religious philosophers have grappled with the morality of a patient's control over his own death. To simplify the ethical imperatives, then, I will focus on DNR orders alone.

The Declaration on Euthanasia affirms that medical decisions that do not offer reasonable hope of benefit or that impose an undue burden on family members may be refused. Of course, the Church makes a moral distinction between excessively burdensome treatment vs. the excessive burdens of a life. To the latter point, euthanasia is not permitted, but DNR orders may be interpreted with a rather wide margin.

Likewise, Talmudic discussions over the permissibility of a patient to refuse treatment has been so extensive and intricate that to summarize even the broadest of them would be an injustice to Jewish medical ethics and philosophy. At the center of the theology lies the concept of intractable pain and suffering and the futility of treating disease with no hopeful outcome. Under these circumstances, patients have autonomy to choose their medical course, but if a cure is guaranteed, the patient may not deter or withdraw therapy.

The Buddhist and Taoist postures on DNR orders reflect a similar stance to those of Christianity and Judaism, although employed less frequently. Both Eastern religions place an emphasis on filial piety, inspiring offspring to provide maximal care for the elderly and possibly influencing some tendency to withhold DNR. Further, these religious teachings may interpret the sufferings of death as a vehicle to gain good karma, which could enhance the likelihood of happiness at rebirth.

Similar consensus has been reached in Islamic law, which stipulates that when resuscitative efforts increase pain, become costly, and prolong the inevitable, DNR orders are encouraged. Defining death becomes problematic for some sects that do not recognize brain death but consider cardiopulmonary death as the only legitimate terminal event.

I first crossed paths with faith and the plea for divine intervention in medical practice in the early months of 1971, when I took a decided departure from the world of science. Between my second and third year, I began an eight-week pediatrics rotation at Guy's Hospital in London. In contrast to American medical students at this level, British students were not required to take night call. Concerned that I would not get to see the entire smorgasbord of childhood diseases during the day, I often chose to stay overnight in the hospital with the registrars (their version of our resident). I imagine the hour must have been close to 2:00 a.m. when I wandered through the neonatal ICU and witnessed the birth of a miracle.

A deep quiet had been gathering in the room as the usual bustle subsided, leaving only the sounds of the rhythmic shushing of mini-ventilators and the soft, high-pitched beeps of heart-rate monitors. The temporary lull in code blues, absence of nurses' shouts for help, and even the brief suspension of the mews of premature babies were a bit disorienting. The thrum and buzz of the sputtering moonlike fluorescent lightbulbs were serene and eerie, reminding me of the Latin root of the word "lunacy." In later years, I would sometimes reflect on the aura of that moment as I read *Goodnight Moon* to my infant children. With one exception, it was as if throughout the entire ICU, a "quiet old lady... was whispering hush." But then I heard a soft mumbling from a corner in the room, gently piercing the silence, a murmur that would have typically been drowned out on any other night but now could be made out distinctly.

I crept up behind the second-year registrar, who was kneeling next to the ventilator of a baby delivered nearly four months premature, the smallest baby yet born at Guy's Hospital. Weighing not much more than ten ounces, her entire body could be cradled in my two cupped hands. The registrar, a member of the Church of Jesus Christ of Latter-day Saints, was calling upon Heaven for a consult. Tears saturating his scrubs, he sobbed and pleaded and prayed with a reverence that could have melted a stone. The solitude, reverence, and sincerity of that moment hung in the air like a night fog.

I tiptoed away, respecting the privacy of the privileged dialogue between the registrar and his Maker. In my limited dictionary of science and medicine, these intimate conversations represented a foreign language that required time to process and translate. Later, I would come to appreciate that similar communications took place far more frequently than I had imagined.

During the next few tenuous weeks, and again a few months later after my return to the States, I checked in on the progress of the frail angel in the corner bassinet. The registrar remained confident that his celestial petitions would be answered. Six months passed before I learned about the divine intervention that delivered this baby from her expected demise. After discovering the registrar's intercession, the little girl's family reinforced their own religious practices. Steadfast in their reinvigorated belief, they watched her grow strong enough to be baptized. They named her Faith.

The metrics used to weigh the role that faith plays in a positive outcome are challenging to quantify. What stretches credulity to a lesser degree, however, is the value that deep-seated belief systems offer to a family or patient grappling with impending death. For families of faith, the trauma of dealing with a loved one's transition can be dramatically blunted. Even as an insignificant student huddled in the shadow of my attending, I could easily sense how that faith can buoy a family's spirits just as it can provide some composure for the patient.

THE SCIENCE OF SOUL-SEARCHING

A SINCERE AND FIRM KNOWLEDGE that death is merely part of a cycle that ends in a defined celestial destination provides enormous comfort for those whose religion promises a haven in Heaven. Conceiving of the soul using anthropomorphic imagery lends shape to the shapeless and concrete to the abstract. Near-death experiences have added "substance" to the faithful's interpretation of the afterlife. During my school years, several patients who had hovered at the threshold of death during their successful resuscitation reported eerily similar visions. Each described a bright light, and many felt a fuzzy interaction, almost a beckoning from loved ones who had died years earlier. It was not my place to engage in a debate that inserted science into the picture or proposed a control experiment; even winning such an argument would have been Pyrrhic. Right or wrong, no harm was done by leaning on a mechanism that helped to ease pain.

Science has, however, probed the meaning of the precise visions patients describe at these pivotal crossroads. One study involved a patient who had arrested in the emergency room. Upon reawakening, he described the sensation of his soul floating in the room as if waiting for the outcome to be determined. While "observing him" during this out-of-body event, his soul was also able to survey the room. The patient recounted how his soul could see the exact shade of an orange tie worn by one of the ER doctors who had stopped by his gurney briefly after CPR had already begun but left before the patient regained consciousness. In other words, there would have been no way for the patient to have seen the orange tie before he had become comatose; presumably, the tie was only "seen" by his soul.

Challenged by this description, a psychiatrist fastened a slide projector upside down to the ceiling of the room in which most resuscitations were performed. The projector was positioned to shine a color close to the ceiling in such a way that it would not be visible from below but could be seen by a "soul" hovering in the room. The color was changed every few hours. Over the next months, many patients had been successfully brought back to life in that room, and many had described their souls temporarily leaving their bodies, but none were able to accurately identify the color projected from the ceiling at that time. The study implied that having heard similar accounts of the soul and lights and family long departed, patients had ample input to construct these visions from what they imagined they should be experiencing—reinforced by a longing for proof of an afterlife that relies on a shared faith. Failing to actually study these auras described by those who "return from the dead" using a controlled experimental model could leave patients, physicians, and clergy conflicted. The power of suggestion is a formidable force; consider its corollary, the placebo effect.

Studies have consistently demonstrated that the placebo effect accounts for a positive response to therapy in roughly 35 percent of patients. By itself, this represents a powerful antidote, although many of the faithful prefer to attribute the secret sauce to the power of prayer. In a study of 1,700 elderly patients, the control group exhibited significantly higher levels of the stress hormone cortisol and interleukin (IL-6, a prominent factor in the response to, and production of, inflammation) than those measured in patients who engaged in regular spiritual practice. Churchgoers tend to live longer and experience less stress. Among hospitalized patients, prayer is the adjunct most often called upon to control pain (76 percent) when compared with intravenous meds (66 percent), intramuscular injections (62 percent), or relaxation methods (33 percent). While one can only assume that the index population's demographics plays a role in determining the consistency of these numbers, in almost any environment, prayer remains a factor of primary significance.

Regardless of their religious upbringing, most medical students who must face patients with terminal illness naturally view this dying as threatening their own sensibility and emotional safe space. And so, less out of indifference or lack of empathy but to mitigate psychic pain, some students avoid contact with the terminally ill. I have seen some students (and attendings) reinterpret the term *DNR* to mean "do not round," bypassing a hospital room and scribbling something in the chart while feeling awkward, guilty, and fragile. I was not immune to that temptation, but I soon realized that to accompany a dying patient on his transcendent journey was a way for me to better understand and appreciate my own life.

A University of Pennsylvania study showed that two-thirds of all patients and 83 percent of patients contemplating life-threatening disease want their doctors to ask them about their spiritual needs. In a 2018 study, 64 percent of doctors and 90 percent of patients professed a belief in a higher power; in a 2004 article published in the *Journal of Thoracic and Cardiovascular Surgery*, 74 percent of 1,100 doctors believed medical miracles had previously occurred.

As a student, I appreciated that there would be definite moments when medicine and faith conflicted. I quickly came to understand the very real difference between a doctor *hoping* for a miracle and a doctor *depending* on a miracle. The *International Archives of Internal Medicine* interviewed twenty-one doctors regarding their attitudes toward patients with spiritual practices, and the doctors' reactions had a lot to do with where the patients were on the devotional spectrum, breaking down into roughly three categories.

The typical first category might include a patient who is a Jehovah's Witness who objects to accepting a blood transfusion. Many of the physicians interviewed might have harbored significant disagreement with this stance, but most recognized the religious imperative. They bowed to the rights of a patient's faith and acquiesced to the decision to abjure treatment.

The second group dealt with patients who held a different world view: "Life in any form is better than death." In this example, a patient sustains irrevocable brain damage requiring mechanical ventilatory support and intravenous drips to maintain a heartbeat and blood pressure. Here, friction arises when the definition of death from a medical standpoint differs from that characterized by religious doctrine. The doctor needs some skill and the family needs some faith to arrive at and adopt a plan that fits both definitions. The challenge to identify common ground is not trivial, and a substantial number of physicians in this study could not meet consensus with families.

The third category involved the dilemma in which prayer alone is preferred as a sole substitute for a known medical cure. In this scenario, essentially all doctors responded emphatically, frustrated by the possibility of being asked to reject therapy that was evidence-based in favor of accepting an unproven alternative. To a large extent, this option was interpreted as a form of reckless abandonment.

As a professor of mine once reasoned, "A cure is not always possible, but there is always room for healing." Early in my medical education, I came to concede that for some, faith facilitates the acceptance of illness, not so much with resignation but with a sense of peace. "Man is not destroyed by suffering," Viktor Frankl wrote in his Holocaust memoir, *Man's Search for Meaning*, "he is destroyed by suffering without meaning."

There is no convincing, controlled experiment that proves that God heals; studies simply show that faith provides for a longer life, better coping mechanisms, improved quality of life, less anxiety and depression, and fewer suicides. Beyond the need to establish causality, eclipsing the contrivances of scientific studies, and even overcoming the swells of a doctor's ego, the manipulation of pain, disease, and death through faith deploys a powerful adjunct to the practice of medicine.

CHAPTER 22

TRENDING NOW: THE WRAP-UP

LOOKING BACK TO THE BEGINNING of my medical training in 1968, I would have found it challenging to predict the status of medical education, the innovations in technology, or the trends in modern medicine that would emerge in the first quarter of the 21st century. This failure should not come as a surprise. You may remember the fad of the early 1950s in which time capsules were deposited into the base of prominent buildings under construction. Futurists from all walks of life—scientists, sociologists, demographers, historians—assembled their hopes, dreams, and predictions for world progress, expecting their forecasts would be revealed when the capsules were opened in seventy-five to a hundred years. Their first prophecy, of course, was incorrect; no one waited that long. As even nearly contemporary buildings were demolished to satisfy presumed American progress, many capsules were violated after just thirty to fifty years. The optimistic seers had embraced a lofty expectation that innovations would solve global societal problems. Regrettably, it was all too evident that was not the case: nuclear weapons had not been banned, the seas not farmed to eradicate world hunger, peace not secured, the environment not safeguarded, racism not abolished, and infection not annihilated.

A Short Lens into the Future

This book was written with two goals in mind.

The first was to provide a glimpse into the lives of medical students as they travel through tragedy and triumph to be molded into the physicians one encounters in offices and hospitals. But their four years of medical school, three years of residency, and up to seven years of subspecialty training must do more than just teach them how to perform surgery, diagnose disease, or order prescriptions.

On the surface, the investment of time seems excessive. Computers and robots could be programmed to be reasonable substitutes for some diagnosis and therapy, and I could probably instruct observant high school students to identify and care for the eight most common uncomplicated reasons that Americans visit their doctors: acne (dermatitis), back pain, arthritis, respiratory infections, headaches, anxiety-depression, high cholesterol, and high blood pressure. But as I have indicated thus far, those efforts would fall short. These long years are designed to teach critical thinking, to provide future doctors with the tools necessary to scrutinize the value or the pitfalls of new ideas, emerging diagnostics, "revolutionary" treatments, or innovative devices. They are vital in crafting scientists, in polishing bedside manner, in teaching compassion, accountability, duty, and service. A computer does not ask a reticent patient an embarrassing question, receive a furtive response, and realize that the answer given is intentionally misleading. A robot does not place a reassuring hand on a shoulder to comfort someone in the presurgical holding unit, allay a loved one's fears, or intuit and untangle convoluted family dynamics.

As the anecdotes I have shared here tell us, *time* is needed to teach and discover the virtues of touch, to appreciate the merits of faith, to grapple with the specter of death, to absorb the noble and elegant art of medicine into one's very pores.

The second goal was to provide insight and a deeper appreciation for the way that regulatory constraints, technological inventions, changes in training programs, and economic pressures have contributed to a paradigm shift in the current doctor-patient experience. Millennials in the medical field have been raised in an environment of instant access. How they amass information—from taking histories to performing physical examinations, from ordering tests to using electronic medical records—translates into a transformative interaction that entails both risk and reward. For the patient, efficiency may be misinterpreted as detachment; for the practitioner, accessibility becomes an intrusion on lifestyle.

A brief diversion from these two goals was designed to address the health of the American health system. All medical systems in the world undoubtedly suffer from imperfections, and ours is no exception, but I've hoped to clarify some of the factors that disturb our satisfaction with American medicine on a personal level and prompt us to pronounce it "broken." Environment, genetics, cultural norms, and even definition, however, also loom as partial root causes for the comparative failure of our healthcare delivery system, although the gaps in wealth, education, and access are undeniable negative forces. Critical analysis of the reasons behind the unfavorable statistics may help direct resources to the places where they will do the most good.

Certainly, trends that seem evident now will almost assuredly be impacted by the dramas of sweeping scientific revolutions and assaults from nature's upheavals. Try to think back just a quarter century to identify which soothsayer could have foretold the enormity of the genome project, the field of the microbiome (the study of the many microorganisms that comprise by far the greatest proportion of the cells in what we think of as the human body), stem cell research, immunotherapy, quantum computing, or a coordinated global effort to attack viral pandemics. So any directional observations you read in this final chapter are likely to be myopic.

Toward More Efficient Doctoring

The tidal wave of medical information is swelling to such heights that despite new learning tools, students will be unable to keep up with the burgeoning data. True, computers can be called upon for instant instruction, but as information about sophisticated pharmacology and insights into health and disease gain complexity, our need to understand them grows exponentially. In the last few decades, the years of subspecialty training has lengthened even further, especially to provide facility and experience to master new techniques. These extra years do not seem sustainable.

One answer is to telescope medical school curricula. Schools will have to acknowledge that every student need not take in-depth courses in, say, pediatrics, obstetrics, surgery, orthopedics, or psychiatry if they plan to pursue fields of interest that will never require that expertise. The information acquired in many arenas during medical school is either quickly forgotten from lack of use or lost to a rapidly evolving science. As a cardiologist in practice after just a few years, I soon learned that I would no longer trust my brief acquaintance with most of these fields to offer opinions on diagnoses or therapies. Embarking on a specialty earlier may allow a student to more carefully choose a study path that reflects future practical needs. Should those interests change, a postgraduate program could supplement or update knowledge already gained. Some schools have already moved in this direction. Specialty training programs must do the same. Every cardiology fellow need not learn how to perform a catheterization or insert a pacemaker if her plan is to become an expert in ultrasound or nuclear medicine.

The science of medicine has widened its shutters to encompass entire fields of engineering, robotics, artificial intelligence, chemistry, and advanced computers. Applications of material science to benefit the sturdiness of coronary stents or cardiac valves, the durability of joint replacements, and the healing of surgical wounds are adding years to the survival of the elderly. Computer technology is vital to the advancement of sophisticated three-dimensional imaging (CT scans, MRIs, nuclear imaging, and ultrasound), digital diabetic feedback monitoring systems, pacemakers and electrophysiology mapping and arrhythmia analysis, cochlear implants, and devices for the visually impaired.

Imagining the brain's ability to fire up to 200 trillion synapses per second as a model, quantum computers are being developed to take on massive data analysis for projects such as artificial intelligence. Robotic surgery currently permits the operator to function from a distance, and on the horizon, an interventional cardiologist will soon be able to insert a stent or replace a heart valve from across the country. Centralizing practitioner expertise could reduce the cost of duplicating expensive facilities as well as the funds needed for patients to travel to centers of excellence. Lost, of course, is the emotional value of direct contact with one's doctor and the additional trust that such a personal interaction catalyzes.

Further applications of distance diagnostics and therapy include a growing spectrum of at-home testing. Companies that have produced kits to test for pregnancy are launching strips that diagnose viral infection and accelerate early cancer detection. More and more, office visits to the doctor will be obviated or shortened through telemedicine. Drones are directed to deliver emergency meds or speed defibrillators to patients who have collapsed in cardiac arrest. Within minutes, resuscitative efforts can be initiated at a beach, in a park, or at home far sooner than by an EMT who waits frustrated in an ambulance snarled in traffic.

The confluence of knowledge surrounding powerful computer analysis and the unraveling of the human genome carries both promise and concern. Given the opportunity to perform "genetic surgery" through CRISPR gene editing, researchers already promise hope to future generations of patients with hemophilia, sickle cell disease, Huntington's chorea, lipid disorders, and other inborn errors of metabolism. The growing field of optogenetics is beginning to treat patients with congenital blindness by activating neurons to become photoreceptors in the eye that respond to light stimulation. The first patients treated with this light-sensitive technique are now beginning to see. Scientists are delivering modified genetic instruction to improve arrhythmic heart cells and injured spinal cords via messenger RNA and up-regulating (promoting) the healing of sick cells and the death of cancer cells. Suddenly, the image of Dr. McCoy from Star Trek passing a light over an injured astronaut's body to promote healing doesn't seem like such science fiction after all.

Geneticists may alter T-cell surfaces to block infectious agents from gaining access to the body, or construct organs for transplantation. But moral questions expose a cautionary tale to those who might use this technology to "order" designer babies with enhanced muscles, intelligence, or beauty. Strict regulatory control may hold the reins in some, but not all parts of the world. One fears that rogue laboratories and clinics may pop up in remote regions, offering "gene tourism" destinations for wealthy prospective parents.

On a more practical note, the delivery of healthcare in the United States is already responding to the pressures of a changing demographic and economy. Physician "extenders," such as nurse practitioners, can play an important role in handling an enlarging number of patients whose wait times to see the doctor would otherwise be unacceptable, if not unnecessary. Follow-up visits and initial screening exams in many specialties relieve the doctor's schedule and promote more prompt throughput. Sadly, for a few physicians, the value of providing this service does not always mirror integrity. I am aware of an internal medicine practice with offices in eight locations operated by dozens of nurse practitioners. The lone physician never sees a patient but simply rubber-stamps hundreds of charts each day. Since typical insurance reimbursements for nurse practitioner visits are roughly 85 percent of a doctor's fees, the doctor's strategy to scale this system is as economically sound as it is ethically flawed. Although placing physician extenders in pharmacies throughout the country also has its benefits, the hidden concern for the select few is the potential to miss serious disease or ensure consistent follow-up or continuity of care. A colleague reminded me of the first words of advice spoken to his class by the chief of medicine: 80 percent of the patients they would evaluate during their careers would either have no real illness or would get better on their own. For the next fifty years, their challenge would be to treat the 20 percent without making the 80 percent worse.

As patients become more used to accepting the notion that medicine is becoming "shift work," they understand that they will not see the same hospitalist each time they are admitted, or even each day of their hospital stay. Students and residents trained with a shift work mentality consider this the new normal—one that offers them a preferred family lifestyle but may not nurture the patient-doctor relationship. What takes place in a hospital setting may soon translate into a team-care approach in the clinic as well.

For the first time as of 2019, more physicians have been employed by hospitals than own their own practices. While referral patterns are still multifaceted, many physicians rely on the hospital or clinic for their patient flow. The clinic "owns" the patient chart and decides on case distribution. Building professional relationships with a wide referral base of colleagues and polishing one's bedside manner to promote a sustainable community outreach are no longer essential for a doctor's practice to survive. That is not to assume that institution-based physicians lack expertise or fail to provide personal care; it simply suggests that the emphasis on these qualities is less critical.

The rush to sell one's practice to a larger hospital network has been spurred by many incentives. Increasing overhead in private offices and declining Medicare reimbursement pose the greatest challenges. Larger doctor networks are more successful in negotiating with third-party carriers, and office management (coding, collections, HR, insurance, equipment purchase and leasing) can be assumed by a central team with an economy of scale. Physicians who retire often have difficulty monetizing their large (and often aging) practices, so "selling" their patients' charts and working for a salary plus incentives gives them an exit strategy that compensates their years of hard work. Medicare payment for services rendered in a private office have typically lagged those given to hospitals for the identical treatment by a significant margin. As the profits shrink for the private sector, many physicians are driven to the security of a large employer, where competition for patient acquisition is not the burden of the individual. Many predict that once a critical mass of practitioners is concentrated in a smaller number of large hospital organizations, Medicare and insurance companies will be able to squeeze reimbursements more effectively.

AFTER THE GLOVES COME OFF: THE PERSONAL TOUCH

IF MEDICAL EDUCATION sacrifices physical contact in favor of technology, the doctor-patient relationship is at risk. Interposing computer tablets or robots to take histories or perform surgery, de-emphasizing physical examination in favor of imaging, relying on electronic medical records to "think their way" through amassing costly diagnostic tests, converting care strategies to conform to shift work, and coalescing private practices into large hospital conglomerates all serve to discourage the personal connection between two people that once was both galvanizing and endearing.

It is no wonder, then, that the appetite for concierge medicine has grown. In a medically complex world, patients fear being herded, marginalized, delayed, and ignored. The terminology doctors use to describe disease is confusing; the diagnostic algorithms are complex, expensive, and sometimes duplicative; and the therapeutic destinations can begin to resemble the map of the Paris Metro. Patients crave a guide. They seek to recapture the personal touch, the demonstration of a doctor's interest they may have experienced in times past. Sadly, the ideal service relationship captured by many concierge practices is accessible only to the few patients who can afford it.

More than ever, swimming against the tide, physicians of the future will have to reconcentrate efforts on honing their bedside manner, developing their intuition, and drawing upon a nuanced understanding of their patients if they are ever to feel the same deep gratification of the profession of their predecessors.

It seems more attractive now than ever before for physicians to free their lives of office management, embrace the safety of employment in a large hospital network, and unwittingly adopt the mechanical mannerisms of the robot-computer partnership they have forged. While the benefits of this new milieu can enhance a doctor's family life and free time, the potential erosion of the patient-physician connection may become even more insidious.

Doctors can counteract this deterioration, recalling the enthusiasm they once felt as premed students contemplating the honor of a future career of service. Recapturing the faith that ignites a spark between two people traveling on a solemn parallel journey ennobles one and enlightens the other. Reflecting on my last fifty years, the ideal balance of fact, faith, and feeling has been elusive. For every practitioner, the ratio of these facets fills the historical reservoir of their medical practice and gives each a personal scope of reference when they look back on their career and consider anew how they have been shaped by their clinical experience.

ACKNOWLEDGMENTS

Precise recollections of events that took place many years ago potentially suffer from subtle but pivotal alterations in fact, nuance, and intention. Distorted further by the ignoble erosions of an aging memory, a memoir faces a significant number of challenges. For lessons to be etched into an impressionable medical student's brain, a certain style of teaching—however severe—has proven valuable, even as it takes a momentary toll on a student's fragile mindset. The reflections of my colleagues described throughout the book bear witness to the enduring power of these experiences. I would like to recall those stressful moments not as sideshows of abuse, but as privileged wisdoms, gifts from the Giants to their students. In the context of "lessons to save lives," the messages were never delivered merely to belittle, but always accompanied a demand to better serve our patients. To that end, during my career, I have tried to put to some use the insightful teachings of my cardiologist-mentors Drs. Eugene Braunwald and Burton Sobel. Their gifts to medical science—the rationale for the development of coronary care units, interventions to limit heart damage during heart attacks, elucidation of mechanisms of heart failure, treatment of valvular heart disease, cardiac genetics, and the training of a huge wave of academic visionaries and clinical cardiologists—all create a legacy that will live on for decades. Learning how to learn by questioning current convention plays an important role in every doctor's ongoing education. That posture, stressed upon us by the Giants, in later years is stimulated by our colleagues. For their encouragement to evolve with modern times and improve as a clinician, I would like to thank the colleagues in my training programs and my partners at Houston Cardiovascular Associates.

This book benefitted enormously from the gentle molding and wise counsel of my editor, Kate Zentall. Technical medical jargon (doctors often seem to speak in Latin) can be ponderous and droll; Kate pushed me to bridge the chasm between physician and reader. I suppose it is not unusual for authors to fall in love with their own writing; Kate cajoled rather than cudgeled to motivate improvement. I would also like to thank Nancy Geyer for her selfless devotion to reading and focusing the book during its earlier phases.

After fifty years of marriage, Gail continues to inspire the "faith and feeling" part of life. Even though I retired from medicine ten years ago, she still prompts me to call and offer support or advice to former patients who are ill, confused, or concerned about their health. Although the science side of medicine is clearly central to its success, Gail's definition of "doctor" spills effortlessly into the humanities and is a constant reminder for me to be more generous with my time.

Thanks also to our sons, Josh and Stephen, for their thoughts on the book and for being the spark that ignited me to be my best. Especially as doctors, we are known by our reputation, and so it is important for me to believe they are proud of my place in their community.

Finally, to those healthcare workers who recognize the dire needs of the people—from the curse of the bubonic plague to the polio epidemic, and from the Spanish flu to COVID-19—we owe enormous gratitude. Many have dedicated their lives, their time, and their intellectual resources to further science and world health. The historical path from hypothesis to thesis and back to hypothesis is rarely smooth and often fraught with public derision. Continuing to press for fact while maintaining faith and feeling can be both a burden and a torch. I am thankful that my predecessors were strong enough to carry the burden and bright enough to be the torch.

www.ingramcontent.com/pod-product-compliance
Lightning Source LLC
Chambersburg PA
CBHW050242010526
44107CB00032B/1380/J